TRANSACTIONS

OF THE

AMERICAN PHILOSOPHICAL SOCIETY

HELD AT PHILADELPHIA

FOR PROMOTING USEFUL KNOWLEDGE

NEW SERIES—VOLUME 53, PART 6
1963

TOLERATION AND DIPLOMACY

THE RELIGIOUS ISSUE IN ANGLO-SPANISH RELATIONS, 1603–1605

ALBERT J. LOOMIE, S.J.

*Assistant Professor of History, Graduate School of Arts and Sciences,
Fordham University*

THE AMERICAN PHILOSOPHICAL SOCIETY

INDEPENDENCE SQUARE

PHILADELPHIA 6

SEPTEMBER, 1963

TO THE MEMORY
OF MY FATHER AND MOTHER

FOREWORD

A century ago, in the first volume of his *History of England,* S. R. Gardiner presented a narrative of the peace negotiations of 1604 between King James I of England and King Philip III of Spain. This reconstruction has been the basis for nearly all subsequent interpretations of that event. There was, however, one major issue which he neglected to explore: the Spanish quest for toleration which formed a part of the secret discussions between both courts for nearly two years. In this study I should like to offer an analysis of this significant diplomatic exchange.

The present inquiry opens with a survey of the reasons which prodded Philip III to intervene on behalf of his coreligionists in England in 1603. In the second chapter the manner of the Spanish approach to King James is explained, and the reasons for its virtual alienation from France and the Papacy at this time are probed. There follows a history of the varied reactions at the English court to the efforts of the envoy, Don Juan de Tassis, to secure a promise of toleration. In the fourth chapter the decisions reached during the visit of the Constable of Castile to England are appraised. After this there is a study of the breakdown of subsequent efforts to reach a satisfactory solution during the last months of the embassy of Tassis. Finally there is an attempt to place this negotiation in the perspective of contemporary history.

My debt is heavy to Sir John Neale and Professor Joel Hurstfield, who guided and encouraged my work as their student in the Tudor seminar at the Institute of Historical Research at London. I am grateful also to Dr. Louis B. Wright and the offer of a summer Fellowship at the Folger Library where this study was completely revised. To the staffs of the archives and libraries where I have discovered the major portion of my documentation—the Archivo General de Simancas, the Public Record Office, and the British Museum—I should like to return sincere thanks for the many courtesies I received.

A. J. L.

Fordham University

ABBREVIATIONS

A.G.R.   Archives Générales du Royaume (Brussels)

A.H.N.   Archivo Historico Nacional (Madrid)

A.R.S.J.   Archivum Romanum Societatis Jesu

A.S.V.   Archivio Segredo di Vaticano

B.M.   British Museum

Correspondencia: A. Rodriquez Villa, *Correspondencia de la Infanta Archduquesa Doña Isabel Clara Eugenia.*

C.R.S.   Catholic Record Society

Cal. S.P.   Calendars of State Papers

Documentos Inéditos: Duque de Alba, ed. *Documentos Inéditos para la Historia de España.*

E   Sección de Estado, Archivo General de Simancas, cited by legajo and carpeta.

Frangipani Correspondence: A. Louant and L. van der Essen, eds. *Correspondence d'Ottavio Miro Frangipani.*

H.M.C.   Historical Manuscripts Commission

Lonchay & Cuvelier: *Correspondence de la Cour d'Espagne sur les Affaires des Pays Bas au XVIIe siècle.*

n.f.   Unnumbered folio in volume or legajo.

P.E.A.   Papiers d'Etats et Audience

P.R.O.   Public Record Office

W.C.A.   Westminster Cathedral Archive

Winwood Memorials: Edmund Sawyer, ed. *Sir Ralph Winwood, Memorials of Affairs of State in the Reigns of Queen Elizabeth and King James I.*

RATES OF EXCHANGE

In references to Spanish coinage, the following brief table of exchange values in contemporary money may be of assistance:

Spain	England
1 ducat	5s. 6d.
4 ducats	£1 2s.

(From "Rates between the monies of England and those of Ireland, Flanders, France and Spain," May, 1582, P.R.O. S.P.12/153/82.) The greatest fluctuations in money occurred over promissory notes and bills of exchange, and not in minted coins, except of course when coins were debased in content. The "felipe" was a ducat valued at $2\frac{1}{2}$ Brabant florins (Lonchay & Cuvelier 1: p. 127). For other Spanish coins see M. Hutchinson, *The School of Salamanca: Readings in Spanish Monetary Theory.*

TOLERATION AND DIPLOMACY

The Religious Issue in Anglo-Spanish Relations, 1603–1605

ALBERT J. LOOMIE, S.J.

CONTENTS

I. THE CONSCIENTIOUS HAPSBURG, 1598–1603

The succession of James of Scotland to the throne of England was viewed with a deceptive indifference from within the austere calm of the Escorial. It was not until April 29, 1603, that Philip III of Spain approved the text of the instructions for Don Juan de Tassis for his embassy to England. Among the foreign ambassadors in Spain there was little excited speculation over his itinerary, which was known to lead northward to Brussels and then, on an as yet undecided date, across the narrow seas. Officially, Tassis was to convey greetings to a new monarch, James I. Technically, Spain and England remained at war, but a cease fire had been declared, and diplomatic courtesy required a state visit and public recognition of the new ruler.

Yet this apparently modest mission to England had a remarkable, though still undisclosed, objective. Prominent in the text of the King's first instructions for Tassis was a bald request to secure toleration for the Catholics of England. King Philip was about to initiate a sustained diplomatic effort which might have placed the subsequent treaty of London in 1604 on a par with the Edict of Nantes. Whatever its merits in other respects, it would be a landmark of civil toleration for different beliefs.

However, unlike Henry IV of France, Philip III was assuming a far different pose. He would be, for many, an interloper in English domestic affairs. The role of a mediator for an oppressed minority was apparently his only reasonable justification. Obviously King Philip hoped to succeed, nor was his interest in this goal bogus, much less, superficial. Yet he failed largely through misinformation from various sources, a mistake compounded by the method his envoy had to use later in England. Only the secrecy surrounding the intrigue prevented the loss of prestige that would have been an obvious penalty after such an intervention. The historical reconstruction of an insignificant diplomatic vignette may be of questionable value, but the appraisal of Philip's failure is essential for understanding the complete pattern of seventeenth-century diplomacy. It was unique in being one of the rare attempts to negotiate a basic emotional and cultural, as well as political, disagreement between states, and it throws light upon the persistent diplomatic tensions existing between the two monarchies.

The degree of concern which the Spanish Hapsburgs bestowed on religious issues in the planning of their diplomatic or military policies has remained one of the more elusive problems in the political history of the "Counter Reform." It has long been discussed, for example, whether the contemporary fanfaronades of crusading propaganda accompanying Philip II's campaigns against the Dutch Calvinists, or his intervention in France on behalf of the League, were merely a convenient boast.[1] The consensus of contemporaries, and of later historians, has been that political, military, or economic advantages loomed larger in the calculations of the Spanish court. This is not to question Philip II's integrity, it is rather to recognize that heresy was abhorred largely as a threat to the unity or safety of the Spanish monarchy.

However, by the turn of the century continental Europe was changing. Religious conformity was being successfully challenged by many dissenting minorities. In Poland, the Holy Roman Empire, Hungary, France, and the Low Countries nonconformity was being permitted in various ways. Toleration had come as a grudging response to various political, intellectual, and economic issues that joined the clamorous chorus of "reasons of state." In effect, the agreements announced at Augsburg in 1555, or at Nantes in 1598, were compromises hammered out, more out of weariness than good will, but always from political necessity.[2]

---

[1] L. van der Essen, "Croisade contre les hérètiques, ou guerre contre les rebelles," *Revue d'Histoire Ecclesiastique* **51** (1956): 56 ff.

[2] See also J. Lecler, *Histoire de la Tolérance au siècle de la Réforme* 2: 411–418. In a region where conformity was still exacted, the political reason for it was implicitly acknowledged. For example, Philip II wrote to Christian IV of Denmark in 1587: "If it is evident that other sovereigns do not permit their subjects to have another religion than that which they possess

This was not unexpected. A monarchy that had chosen religious unity as one prop for survival could also subsequently opt for religious diversity out of necessity. For example, Henry IV of France was the realist at Nantes. He maintained the unity of his kingdom while guaranteeing the Catholic position, quieting the *politiques,* and offering *amendes* to his former Huguenot supporters. Despairing of religious unity, he settled for *"un roi, une loi, mais pas une foi."* Yet he acted without the approval of the mass of Catholics and the support of the Hugenot leaders. He was intent on internal peace and the augmentation of his royal prerogatives;[3] he was to reach these goals with little difficulty.

Thus, in an era where religious issues had a clear contemporary urgency, a monarch was rarely to be found taking unnecessary risks on their behalf. Altruism, or compassion, was a luxury in the face of a nation's political or economic priorities. An attempt to make a religious issue coincide with them was rarely successful. The analysis of the history of Philip III's relations with English Catholicism will afford a unique opportunity to explore why this was so.

The decision of Philip to negotiate on the question of toleration involved certain obvious risks. At the English court there was a familiar suspicion that his concern over the Catholics was only a thinly disguised gambit for nurturing a Spanish faction during the war. Don Juan de Tassis, his envoy, would be later accused of setting religion as a lure for the unsuspecting towards another allegiance. If viewed from the first as a Trojan horse, Tassis' objectives could be branded as subversive to England's national interests. With these hobbling suspicions poised to ensnare the steps of the Spanish envoy, a fundamental problem appeared. What were King Philip's real reasons for intervening at all? In order to appreciate the depth of Philip's commitment to the toleration issue his previous handling of the English Catholic problem must be surveyed.

When Philip had come to the throne in September, 1598, there were unfavorable auguries over his ability to handle the complexities of his realms on the continent and overseas. He could not have been aware of his father's impatient prediction of a lacklustre future to a favorite councilor: "God has given me so many kingdoms, but not a son fit to govern them."[4] Although Spain had patched up a peace with Henry IV at Vervins in the spring of 1598, the financially exhausting war with the United Provinces and England was continuing without any prospect of a quick settlement. Moreover, the audacity of Barbary pirates,

Dutch contraband traders, and English privateers was reaching even to the coastal waters of Spain. The bankruptcy of 1577 had been repeated at the Spanish court only a year before Philip III's accession. While these troubles could be exaggerated by an alarmist anxious to discern the omnious signs of a perennial historical enigma: "the decline of Spain," Philip had come to the throne at a time when Spanish achievements had, at best, reached a plateau. It was clear that the monarchy had been showing a marked inability to continue the memorable successes of a preceding generation.

Burdened with such an inheritance at the age of twenty, Philip tried, with more credit than has usually been conferred, to secure better administrative talent. His first appointments were, on the whole, perceptive.[5] Of greater significance was to be his clear preference for peace and diplomacy, which was motivated in part by real conviction, in part by economic necessity. Spain could no longer afford the luxury of war as an instrument of diplomacy. The first years of his reign were to show him to be a diffident, cautious, yet conscientious apprentice in kingship; neither as aggressive and adroit as Henry IV, nor as hard headed and wary as the veteran Elizabeth. There was one trait of the young King's rule which was also emerging: he could show, like his father, patience and stubbornness when he had finally decided upon a course of action.

At first the most tangible demonstration of Philip's interest in English Catholicism had been his continuance of his father's generosity towards the English refugees in his lands. He gave funds to the maintenance of the colleges for young English students in Valladolid, Seville, Douai, and St. Omer. He also ordered pensions to be given to scores of new English exiles for various services, principally through the accounts of the Spanish army in Flanders.[6] At the turn of the century a number of these English Catholics were still being encouraged to write the apologias and theological and devotional tracts that were to become a part of the typical recusant library in seventeenth-century England.

These solid compassionate gestures on the part of the Spanish Hapsburgs had inevitably aroused hopes for grander assistance. The clear indifference of Catherine de Medici, and, at first, of Henry IV left Spain as the only hope of the English Catholics in their efforts to find relief from the penal laws. Eventually, in the latter part of the reign of Elizabeth, it was to be a bromide of the political tracts of the day to denounce the ominous intercourse between the "papist" and Spain.[7]

However, the relationship of the Spanish court to the

---

themselves, both for reasons of state and religious motives, why is that attitude forbidden to me?" (Cited in L. van der Essen, *Alexandre Farnese* **5**: 78.)

[3] See G. Rothrock, "Some Aspects of Early Bourbon Policy Towards the Huguenots," *Church History* **29**(1960): 17–24.

[4] Matias Novoa, "Memorias o Historia de Felipe III," *Colección de Documentos Inéditos* **60**: pp. 36 ff.

[5] See the revisionist opinion of Ciriaco Perez Bustamente, *Felipe III Semblanza de un monarco y perfiles de una privanza* (Madrid, 1950), p. 47 ff.

[6] A. J. Loomie, *The Spanish Elizabethans: Studies in the English Exiles at the Court of Philip II* (New York, 1963), chap. 2 and 6.

[7] J. E. Neale, *Elizabeth I and Her Parliaments* **2**: pp. 172–173, 372–373, 423–424.

English refugees was not necessarily harmonious or satisfying. Inevitably the latter were so preoccupied with the survival of their faith at home under the mounting repression of the more recent recusancy laws, that they were impatient with Philip III's concentration on the lethal threat to the Hapsburg hegemony in the Low Countries. Yet the efforts of the exiles to increase his concern about England, notably in the final years of Elizabeth's reign, did have one significant result. In agitating for a Catholic contender to the throne of England, they also created a groundswell of discussion on the possibility of toleration which finally touched the King.

The succession to the throne of England had become undoubtedly the most urgent issue in the final melancholy years of the great queen. Previously Elizabeth had successfully enforced her prohibition of any public discussion of her successor, while her hostility to any "sun rising" had never been concealed. However, the English exiles in their safe haven on the continent had clarified in print their basic approach to the unusual situation that the death of the last of the Tudors would present. Historically each Tudor had represented a new orientation of the English crown's policy towards Catholicism. The orthodoxy of Henry VII had given away to the uncertainties of the schism of his son, while under Edward were introduced many of the typical features of continental Protestantism. The short-lived and unsubstantial restoration of Catholicism under Mary [8] had all too easily succumbed to the will of Parliament and the young Queen to reestablish the basic Protestantism of Edward. Thus at the turn of the century the Catholic contemporaries of the aging Elizabeth could find in the previous zigzags of religious opinion at the English court a basis for reasoning that the status quo need not necessarily endure under a new ruler.

The Conference about the Next Succession which appeared in Latin and English in 1595 was a cooperative discussion by some of the leading refugees in Spanish Hapsburg territories [9] on this momentous political and religious issue. Its closely reasoned theme was that the history and laws of the western monarchies did not require "nearness of blood" as the unique norm of rightful succession. It pleaded that religious orthodoxy could be joined to blood with equal justice, and then scrutinized critically eleven contenders for the throne of England in an effort to find a suitable claimant.

The book had immediate repercussions. It was quickly—if inaccurately—assumed by many to be only a clever trick for promoting the chances of the Infanta Isabella Clara Eugenia for the throne.[10] Philip II was

as taciturn as ever over this novel, and unexpected, invasion by the exiles of his control of policy. He did not declare her rights even when, a year later in the summer of 1596, a few of the prominent English refugees in Spain petitioned him pointedly "to take in hand" the problem "as warmly as it deserves," to weigh the import of his daughter's claims and to solicit strong support from the Papacy.[11] Instead King Philip began to complete his grand design to betroth the Infanta to her cousin, the Archduke Albert, the Governor of the Low Countries and to arrange for the transferral to them of the sovereignty of those provinces.

In this haphazard fashion the will-of-the-wisp of the candidacy of the Infanta for the throne of England began to be blown about the courts of Europe. Neither King Philip nor the Infanta encouraged it, but in their inactivity they never showed the statesmanship to quash the refugees' expectations. Yet there were many fitting opportunities to make clear their policy. For example, on August 27, 1597, Father Joseph Creswell informed King Philip II that "the Catholics of England" were pleased with the news of his daughter's betrothal. He noted, however, that "they humbly entreat your Majesty to order the donation of your own rights to that crown (of England) to her Highness, so as to avoid the troubles and occasions of war." [12] Philip still did nothing. Eight months later a group of four leading refugees approached the Archduke Albert in Brussels. They reminded him that "everything depends on the presence of the Infanta in the Low Countries . . . on her arrival she must publicly proclaim her title; books about it must be printed in various languages." [13] Again nothing happened, for the lingering last illness of the King excused many decisions.

It was only natural that Philip III, in the midst of his preoccupation with the momentous problems of his newly inherited empire, should at first have viewed the debates and petitions of the English exiles on the succession issue with a puzzled reserve. It was not until January, 1600, that an earnest inquiry from the Spanish court was made in Brussels over the chances of the Infanta as a candidate. The response from the Archduke Albert was not encouraging, nor, at the outset, was that of the ambassador, Don Baltazar de Zúñiga.[14] Yet Philip still did not clarify publicly his policy. He continued to give private assurances of interest, and he permitted the ambiguity surrounding the candidacy of the reluctant Infanta to stay as a lure for the speculations of the English refugees. Her claims were also discussed, undoubtedly by their com-

[8] See the conclusion of A. G. Dickens, "The Marian Reaction in the Diocese of York," *St. Anthony's Hall Publications* nos. 11 and 12 (1957).

[9] L. Hicks, "Robert Persons and the Book of Succession," *Recusant History* 4 (1957) : 106–107, 110–113.

[10] J. B. Black, *The Reign of Elizabeth* (2nd ed.), pp. 446–447.

[11] *Cal. S. P. Spanish 1587–1603*, pp. 636–637.

[12] E 178 n.f. autograph letter.

[13] Sir William Stanley, Richard Stanyhurst, Hugh Owen and Father William Holt signed the letter of 3 May, 1958. E 2288 n.f.

[14] E 616/182; E 2224(2)/1, 2, dispatches of 18 and 29 January, 1600.

patriots in England. Yet was this vapid policy supported by the Spanish Council of State?

The sentiments of some of Philip's advisers were anything but vague. For example, the advice of the second Duke of Feria on this issue was both perceptive and significant. As the son of Lady Jane Dormer, a former lady-in-waiting to Mary Tudor, and an experienced Spanish envoy and administrator, Feria knew and admired several prominent refugees. Early in 1600 he decided to warn one of his friends, Thomas Fitzherbert: "If our king were capable of doing something, I might, in other circumstances, have different advice, yet the Council must take into consideration the way matters are now arranged." [15] Feria had put his finger on the problem. Since too little military and diplomatic support could be spared for the undertaking why continue to pursue the question? He advised instead that both Philip and the English Catholics should cultivate King James VI so that, as he put it, "that king will be under an obligation." It was admitted by all that the war with England was a great obstacle in the whole problem. The Duke of Sessa reported from Rome in the following April that "the Catholics wish for peace in the hope that, when your Majesty has an ambassador appointed for England, he can deal with things more fully, especially that which touches the future succession." [16]

This attitude of the English Catholics had clearly been prompted by the hopeful news of negotiations for peace which were to begin at Boulogne in the early summer of 1600. However, the commissioners from England, Spain, and the Archduke were soon to be deadlocked over precedence and the agenda of the conference. The promising situation of the spring evanesced. The English Catholic exiles, who looked reluctantly on any other candidacy, continued to rely on Spain until they would be definitely rebuffed. It was not until February, 1601, that Philip III finally rewarded their patience. In a letter to the Duke of Sessa in Rome he confided: "Having considered the matter, and recommended it earnestly to God, I have decided that the succession to that kingdom ought to be procured for the said Infanta." [17]

It was an elusive victory. The King issued surprisingly furtive instructions to communicate this explicit declaration to only a selected few, "for harm might result from it being generally known." The spark that had ignited the damp tinder of Philip's velleity at this time was a tentative feeler from certain English courtiers who were clearly curious over the real strength of Philip's determination on the succession.[18] However, the intransigence of the Infanta and the Archduke against any public announcement for or against her candidacy, the previous commitment of Philip's treasury to other projects of immediate priority, the gradual forging of a close, secret bond between King James and the gifted Sir Robert Cecil were all to deprive Philip's tardy decision of any serious effects.

Inevitably the ambiguous and unhelpful stand adopted by Philip III for over two years was to prove exasperating to many English exiles. Some deserted the faction devoted to the fruitless candidacy of the Infanta. From Rome, Father Robert Persons wrote to Don Baltazar de Zúñiga in Brussels suggesting that the only suitable thing to do was to have Spain make peace with England. He advised that the quest for toleration should be abandoned for the present so that later a resident ambassador could deal with toleration and the succession more conveniently.[19] This useful suggestion would certainly have improved Philip's actual experience of English politics and the nuances of the Catholic question there. The advantage of an official observer in London would have eliminated partially the suspicion that the exiles were indulging in special pleading.

However, King Philip was stubborn and blunt in his refusal to consider negotiations with Queen Elizabeth. Apparently he was not disturbed so much at the prospect of failing to prevail over English arms; what he strongly objected to was that such an approach would be the abandoning of one of the vital principles of the Spanish monarchy. On June 2, 1601, he rejected the suggestion of Robert Persons which had been endorsed by a *consulta* of the Council of State. He wrote: "For no cause may the point of religion be omitted, since all the reasons which maintain me, and the realms which God has given me, depend on it." [20]

A significant comment indeed. The refusal of the Infanta and the Archduke to consider the candidacy was now matched by the inflexibility of Philip over abandoning—even for a time—the point of religion in reaching an understanding with England. The immobility of Philip's policy was now complete. The King's failure to offer any alternative advice to the exiles made them partners in a stalemate created by his evasions. He did not look with favor on any step towards approaching King James; he was still carefully encouraging the impression that their confidence in him would be eventually rewarded. At the English court, Thomas Phelippes, Cecil's clever decipherer, aptly described Spain's policy in his review of intercepted letters: "The King of Spain can not do the enterprise of England as he would, and will not as he may." [21]

For the rest of Elizabeth's lifetime the probability of Spain's success in dealing with either the succession or toleration did not alter. The question remained in the doldrums. The only relief in this gloomy prospect was

[15] W.C.A. Series E vol. ii f. 132, letter of February 4, 1600.

[16] E 972 n.f. dispatch of 19 April, 1600.

[17] E 1856 n.f. letter of 12 February, 1601.

[18] The full correspondence is available in L. Hicks, "Sir Robert Cecil, Father Persons and the Succession," *Archivum Historicum Societatis Iesu* **24** (1955) : 21 ff.

[19] E. 618 n.f. dispatch from Brussels, 1 May, 1601.

[20] E 2023/48. A *consulta* was the written opinion of the Council of State upon a question of policy proposed by the King.

[21] *Cal. S.P. Dom. 1598–1601*, p. 460.

the occasional flickerings of interest at the Spanish court over a promising *détente* between Henry IV and Philip III, which, however, never passed the stage of discussions.

By August, 1602, as the hopes of the exiles foundered on the inability of Philip to fashion any new policy, there was a wistful appraisal of the real cause of the impasse in a personal letter of Robert Persons to King James: "I do assure your Majestie in all sinceritie, that if the former difference of religion were not, or had not byn, or might be hereafter removed, . . . no man living would be more readie to spend his blood for your Majestie and his service than myselfe. . . ."[22]

Yet the effect of this failure on King Philip was not to be ignored. He realized, and admitted at the time of King James' accession, that he had wasted nearly four years giving private assurances to the English Catholics to trust in him.[23] Yet nothing substantial in war or diplomacy had been accomplished, would the time for action ever come?

The spring of 1603 was not a propitious time for Philip to approach the English Catholic question. Neither the Archduke Albert, nor Pope Clement VIII, nor King Henry IV was truly sympathetic to, or even fully aware of, the new calibre of Philip's designs. The basic reasons for this unsatisfactory state of affairs was that the mutual suspicions of these Catholic princes built up over four years were not being sufficiently allayed. Philip's troubles with the Archduke stemmed largely from the latter's identification with the independent-minded Flemish nobility at his court, who were mistrusted by Spain. In a letter from Brussels, Don Baltazar de Zúñiga had epitomized this Castilian incompatibility when he warned: "Although they are Catholics . . . they have been brought up among heretics and they do not have the same integrity in matters of religion, nor that interest in its preservation and increase, as those who are born where that is foremost."[24] This regrettable misalignment of outlook had spread to all problems of diplomacy to such a degree that on one occasion Philip III pointedly advised Don Baltazar to remind the Archduke that "he was not to have other friends nor other enemies" than those of Spain.[25]

The poor relations of Spain with France and the Papacy were more indelible as they were a legacy of the frustrations of Philip II's ambitions in France in 1593 as well as several later clashes in northern Italy. The Constable of Castile, who was a member of the Council of State in 1603 and later to be Philip's official envoy for the ratification of the treaty of London, had been Governor of Milan when Clement VIII had ordered papal troops to occupy the Duchy of Ferrara in the autumn of 1597. On that occasion, when Spain's bankruptcy had prevented the Constable from enforcing Milan's claims to the area, he complained bitterly to Philip II that Pope Clement was "by nature prejudiced in favor of France, for he loves the Bearne, as his own son and creature." He charged that the Pontiff had "on many occasions shown little good will towards your Majesty's plans, for he is displeased with your kingdom's greatness. The man is at a heart a Florentine."[26]

Within the tradition of the Spanish court's attitude to France remained a cynical view of Henry's opportune conversion. Philip, not unexpectedly, looked upon any cooperation with France as reaching for the long spoon "to sup with the devil." Even during his dilatory diplomacy over a Catholic candidacy for the English throne Philip had rarely concealed his dislike of any suggestion of consulting Henry IV. "The King of France has no following in England, nor is the French nation acceptable to the English,"[27] he once warned his envoy in Rome.

In effect King Philip's decision to intervene alone with King James on behalf of toleration was molded by all the nuances of his previous frustrations with the problem of the English Catholics. Fretting over the memory of his miscalculations in the succession issue and his chagrin at the unfulfilled assurances that the English had best rely upon him, he believed they still awaited his aid. Success could bring their lasting gratitude. What was still missing? An accurate appraisal of the politics of the English court under its new ruler, and an appreciation of the varying reactions of Brussels, Paris, and Rome to the new monarch across the channel. In the coming weeks, while new information was assessed by the King of Spain and his Council of State, the precise instructions for Don Juan de Tassis could be prepared.

II. THE PLAN TAKES SHAPE, MARCH–AUGUST, 1603

A recent historian of the most dramatic battle of the Anglo-Spanish war has observed: "the defeat of the Spanish armada was a decisive battle . . . but there is much less agreement as to what it decided. It certainly did not decide the issue of the war between England and Spain."[1] After 1588 the war had continued spasmodically on land and sea for nearly fifteen years until the complex original motives that had started it were blurred and nearly forgotten. The Spanish monarchy had made no headway against England, yet it was not seriously wounded, and the Indies were still accessible only to the occasional hardy English privateer. The Low Countries were already being split by

---

[22] Stonyhurst MS. Anglia III f. 20 letter of 16 August, 1602.
[23] *Cal. S.P. Spanish 1587–1603*, pp. 720, 726, 730.
[24] E 2288 n.f. dispatch of 12 January, 1600.
[25] Lonchay & Cuvelier, 1: p. 73.

[26] F. Braudel, *La Mediterranée et le Monde Mediterranéen à l'époque de Philippe II,* pp. 1069-1070.
[27] E 187 n.f. letter to Sessa, 3 September, 1601.
[1] G. Mattingly, *The Armada,* p. 397.

the fortunes of war, and the benefits of geography, into two parts: an independent and officially Calvinist north and a Catholic south, which was restless to exploit the autonomy already transferred to Brussels in the summer of 1598. Both combatants were increasingly disturbed at the ambitious initiative of the revived French monarchy of Henry IV.[2]

While the outcome of the war had been frustrating to the war parties in both courts, there was little real hope of a lasting Anglo-Spanish amity until time and diplomacy had been given an opportunity to work their soothing effects. The interests of the combatants—including religious tensions—still begged for negotiation and compromise.

The proclamation of James I as the King of England stimulated different reactions in the courts at Brussels, Rome, Paris, and Valladolid. Not unexpectedly, the exchanges between the Archduke Albert and King James were the more cordial. The Scotsman replied happily from Holy Rood that he was gratified at the friendly gestures of his "cousin," and that there was "nothing closer to his heart" than the renewal of England's ancient friendship with the houses of Austria and Burgundy.[3] Meanwhile the Infanta confided hopefully to the Duke of Lerma that she expected the memory of his mother's death would spur the new King's conversion, towards which, she felt, "strong signs" were pointing.[4]

Philip of Spain was hardly as demonstrative. He permitted his envoy to Henry IV, Don Juan Baptista de Tassis, to offer congratulations to the English ambassador in Paris, while he informed the Archduke merely that he intended for the present to await the turn of events.[5] His personal reaction was revealed to the Duke of Sessa, when he was ordered to review cautiously with the Pope the problems of a peace with England. Sessa was to be careful to mention that assisting the English Catholics was a task "befitting his Holiness," for Philip had "no ambitions" within that kingdom "save what touches religion." He expected, he noted rather slyly, that Pope Clement "would also profit from the advice of the French," for Henry and Philip were agreed that "the King of Scotland" should be obliged to alter the lot of the Catholics.[6]

King Henry, however, had already sensed the new advantages for France in James's peaceful accession. His letter to his envoy in London, the Comte de Beaumont, written when only the news of the Queen's last illness had reached him, expressed the hope that the Catholics would not "irritate" the King of Scotland when he came to the throne.[7] After word of her death had arrived he advised Beaumont to present greetings to James and to urge him to maintain his help of the Dutch. His envoy was also to press discreetly for a new approach to the Catholic problem.[8] It was quite significant that he did not mention any collaboration with Spain in this regard. Already the hope of a *démarche* with Spain on the toleration question had faded. Yet Henry was popular in Rome. It was still evident that Clement VIII would cherish France as his counterpoise to Spain.[9] As a result, the hope of James's clemency to Catholics—or the lure of his possible conversion—still confirmed the Pope in the belief that Spain's diplomatic "enterprise" for toleration would be superfluous. James's erratic record on the question in Scotland had ultimately favored this impression. For he had maintained friendship with several Catholic nobles, even when he had been careful to excuse this attitude to Sir Robert Cecil by confiding: "alas, it is a far more barbarous and stiff-necked people that I rule."[10]

From Rome the reports of the Duke of Sessa confirmed the lack of enthusiasm for Spain's plans about England. In one private audience Pope Clement told Sessa that he expected, "at the least," that James would not be "rigorous" with the Catholics, and that even if he did not grant public toleration he would "dissimulate," as he was already doing with Queen Anne's Catholicism.[11] Three weeks later the Duke noted that the papal court, "in general," believed James would sue for peace, so as to enjoy a neutral position between France and Spain. As far as the toleration question was concerned, however, he noticed disturbing reports that the Archduke would be asked by the new king to close the English colleges in the Low Countries as a price for friendship.[12]

Despite the spate of rumors, James's happy relations with Brussels continued to make the Archduke optimistic. He reported in near triumph that James had assured his envoy, Scorza, in Scotland: "I do not like the Dutch, nor their cause, but tell that to no one." As before, the Infanta continued to write wistfully to the Duke of Lerma: "every day there are greater hopes that he will be a Catholic."[13] Yet the Spanish court remained unmoved in the face of what it considered the *naïveté* of the Archduke. The known hostility of some

---

[2] See R. B. Wernham, "Elizabethan War Aims and Strategy," in *Elizabethan Government and Society,* pp. 340 ff.; P. Geyl, *The Revolt of the Netherlands* (2nd ed.), pp. 233 ff.

[3] Lonchay & Cuvelier, 1: pp. 139–40.

[4] *Correspondencia,* p. 83.

[5] Lonchay & Cuvelier, 1: p. 145.

[6] E 191 n.f. letter of 21 April, 1603, copy.

[7] P.R.O. 31/3/35 letter of 27 March, 1603.

[8] "qu'il soit faict quelque faveur aux Catholiques du pais, affin d'amender aucunement leur condition en ce changement, si faire ce peult." Letter of 14 April, 1603. P. Laffleur de Kermaingant, *L'ambassade de France en Angleterre* 2: p. 107.

[9] Pierre de l'Estoile commented after the death of Clement in March 1605: "Pape pacifique et bon Francais, que était la cause que le Roi l'aimait et l'honorait beaucoup." Michaud & Poujoulat, *Registre-Journal de Henri IV* 15: p. 383.

[10] J. Bruce, *Correspondence of James VI,* p. 31.

[11] E 977 n.f. dispatch of 4 May, 1603.

[12] E 977 n.f. letter of 22 May, 1603.

[13] E 622/42, 47 letters of 30 April; *Correspondencia,* p. 87.

sections of English opinion to the mere rumor of a peace negotiation was making it hesitate even more.

Nineteen years of warfare had fostered in many Englishmen an anti-Spanish sentiment which would be loudly expressed in the early months of James's reign. "The Spanish Empire hath been greatly shaken and hath begun of late years to decline. It is a principle of philosophy . . . that the least decay of any part is a forerunner of the whole . . ." declared Sir Walter Raleigh.[14] He was convinced that further warfare would soon weaken Spain to such an extent that free access to the Indies and the triumph of the United Provinces would be won easily and quickly. His argument was typical of numerous anonymous tracts that were circulated at that time. Since no one knew as yet what sort of peace agreement—if any—was possible between England and Spain, most of the anti-Spanish writers imagined the most disastrous terms that England could receive. The complete end of assistance to the Dutch, for example, was thought to be the most likely. With the Dutch isolated it was easily foreseen that a Spanish "tyranny" with a panoply of Bishops and the Inquisition would soon seize the rebellious Calvinists and subdue them.[15]

In another tract, possibly inspired by Raleigh's, the writer advised King James that England allied with the Dutch would "overthrowe the King of Spain and take his Indies from him" and impose any peace it wished. Moreover, this alliance could enable England "to put a bridle into the mouth of any Prince of Europe"; yet if this alliance collapsed the Spanish would quickly "surprise" the Low Countries for, even alone, Spain had remained "terrible and fearsome to all Christendome."[16]

The very idea of peace to another writer was a violation of a successful Elizabethan policy. James was exhorted to follow the steps of "the late wise and provident Prince and Queen of high memory, Elizabeth," and bind "the Britanische kingdoms" to a league with France and the Dutch to conquer Spain, for "that kingdom has always desired the . . . conquest of England and will use religion to stir up sedition" as it had in the past.[17]

Yet not every part of England could respond to such appeals. The English merchants who had traded with Spain were anxious to recover their former profits. Their motives were understandable. In the preceding decade there had been several bad harvests in England which inflated the price of grain while the war had closed the access to Spanish supplies. The wool trade

with the continent had worsened, and even the returns from privateering were declining as the Spanish convoy system improved. The crown had gone increasingly into debt through the heavy expenses of the campaigns in Ireland and the Low Countries.[18] The dilemma had become plain to James: his need for peace was being countered by popular tracts which championed war, or supported issues which made a treaty a remote possibility. A cease fire was a fragile vessel, all too easily broken. King James could not have been unaware of Philip's interest in toleration. The discussions of the succession issue were too public to have been missed by his unofficial envoys in Rome and Spain. Omitting any reference to what clearly King Philip and the Catholic powers were anxious to learn, he merely announced the end of hostilities.

As King of Scotland he had been at peace with Philip, and he apparently reasoned that this relationship could be transferred to English affairs. Hard on the heels of the proclamation of his accession he announced a cease fire with Spain. To show that he was in good faith two other proclamations were issued. The first canceled all letters of *marque* against Spain, as they were immediately made void by the death of the Queen, and the other summoned home to England all ships at sea that carried them.[19] Significantly, James did not announce any change in the English alliance with the United Provinces, which had been renegotiated at Westminster in 1598, nor was there any reference to the English troops serving with the Dutch in the war against the provinces of the Archduke.

Philip III of Spain had responded to this clear change in English policy by granting English ships access to Spanish ports. On May 11, 1603, the secretary of the Council of State wrote to the *corregidor* of Guipuzcoa that the Spanish system of trading licenses, which was intended to confine its commerce to the Catholic powers and neutrals, was opened also to England. "The King of Scotland has succeeded to the throne of England," he wrote, "and he has always been in friendship with us and is understood to desire to remain so. His Majesty is pleased to command that . . . under the name of neutrals is to be understood the kingdom of England and Ireland, as well as Scotland and Denmark, without exception."[20]

Once James had extended the olive branch by the cease fire, Philip was reluctantly obliged to send an envoy to convey the greetings of the Spanish monarchy. Within a short time the selection of a relatively obscure middle-aged hidalgo had become known at Valladolid. Don Juan de Tassis had been a career servant of the crown, but untried in major diplomatic encounters. His

[14] "Discourse Touching a War with Spain," *The Works of Sir Walter Raleigh* (Oxford, 1829) **8**: p. 299 ff. See also Salyer, *Simancas* **1** (1950) : pp. 371 ff.

[15] Folger Library MS. G.b.8 ff. 39v–43. "A Discourse upon the Kings necessitie to make peace or to keepe warre from Spain."

[16] Folger Library MS. G.a.1 ff. 22–28, 46–47v. "A Discourse against the Peace with Spaine."

[17] Folger Library MS. G.b.8 ff. 44–48v, "Discourse whether it bee fitt for England to make peace with Spayne."

[18] W. R. Scott, *The Constitution and Finance of English, Scottish, and Irish Joint Stock Companies* **1**: pp. 100–102, 129–130.

[19] R. Steele, *Tudor and Stuart Proclamations* **1**, nos. 952, 956.

[20] P.R.O. S.P.94/9/20, see also *H.M.C. Salisbury MS.* **15**: p. 73.

family was far more important than the dossier of his previous services, which were those of a bureaucrat. As a member of the Spanish branch of the Taxis family, he represented a tradition of nearly a century of service to the Hapsburgs in Austria, Flanders, France, and Spain. Don Juan's grandfather, Johann Baptista von Taxis, had built up a rudimentary postal and courier service for Charles V, who granted him the office of *Postmeister*. His uncle, Don Juan Baptista de Tassis, had served in the Low Countries and more recently as a commissioner to the conference at Vervins, after which he had become Spain's envoy to Henry IV. Don Juan's brother, Don Pedro de Tassis, had risen to the post of *Veedor General* in the Spanish army in Flanders. Previous to this appointment as envoy to England, Don Juan de Tassis had been *Correo Major* for Philip III and, since 1599, a court chamberlain. Later during his embassy in England he was to be rewarded with his more familiar title of Count of Villa Mediana.[21]

In the text of his first instructions, which were dated April 29, 1603, Tassis was ordered to proceed to Paris and Flanders before traveling on to England. In Paris he was to consult his uncle, Juan Baptista, over the French reaction to the candidacy of Philip III as King of the Romans, and then to pursue the question more fully with the Archduke. Tassis was also told to keep seeking advice on English affairs among the court officials at Brussels, as well as among the exiles. Philip's words reflect his attitude of begrudging condescension towards the new ruler:

The king of England should see how important it is for his continuance to be in league with me. To this end, you should rally the Catholics of England and Ireland, but do it so that you are, at the same time, assuring the well being of the said Catholics.

He then deliberately reminded his envoy that King James, through an envoy in Rome, Sir James Lindsey, had let it be known in the summer of 1602 that Prince Henry would be brought up a Catholic if Spain would support him for the throne of England.[22] He ignored the fact that Spain had not supported James; it simply had not been able to hinder him. Typically, Philip was conscious of his role of protector of the Catholics when he advised his envoy to help in gaining the support of the Catholics for King James "in return for their complete security in matters of religion." [23]

Tassis was also handed a large packet of letters of introduction to the Archduke and other court officials. In addition there were letters of greetings to members of the English nobility, for, apparently, there were fresh reports declaring them to be well disposed to Spain.

Letters, without precise designation by name, were readied for "10 Dukes, 10 Earls, 30 Barons, 10 Marquisses, 10 Viscounts." A strange and clumsy gesture! It was obviously unknown at the Spanish court that the peerage of England did not contain a duke since 1572, and there was but the single Marquisate of Winchester. Philip's special letter to these nobles was far more interesting. It contained a broad hint about the advantages of Spanish protection. The King wrote that, with the death of Elizabeth, those

who publicly or secretly have kept the Catholic religion in their heart, will have greater need of my patronage and protection, so as to profess it publicly when the occassion offers. . . . I am sending Don Juan de Tassis, my ambassador, that he might learn the state of your affairs. He is to assist in them and you may give complete credit to everything that he might say on my part. You may treat with him freely over what is fitting for the universal good of the Catholics and yourselves.[24]

There was little likelihood that any of these letters were used by Tassis in his encounters with the English nobility later. But the fact that such an apparently naïve, and even dangerous, letter could be prepared finds a partial explanation in the current Spanish opinion of the English court. On March 13, 1603, the Spanish ambassador in Rome, the Duke of Sessa, had sent an urgent and lengthy dispatch to King Philip which arrived at the same time as the news of the death of the English Queen. Sessa reported that in the preceding year, Thomas Sackville, one of the sons of Lord Buckhurst, the Lord Treasurer of England, had journeyed to Italy and after attending lectures at Padua had come to Rome. There he was received into the Catholic Church by Father Robert Persons. The young Englishman had then returned to England where his father had told him to keep the matter secret and had allowed him to return to Italy. On this second trip Sackville brought to the Duke of Sessa a startling and partisan report on the attitude of the Privy Council towards the accession of James. The dispatch did not contain any names of the Councilors but otherwise the report would give reason to any foreign statesman to reflect. "The Councilors of England," Sackville told Sessa,

are very anxious over what is to be done on the succession after the death of the Queen. For, as they are *politiques* and the large part of them are inclined more surely to the Catholics, they have a secret dislike of the king of Scotland. This is partly because he is a puritan, which is a sect very dangerous to the present state of England, and partly because the king and his Scotsmen are quite poor so that they fear they will alter their fortune with the goods of Englishmen, and finally because that King shows slight loyalty and faith in keeping his word.[25]

Thomas Sackville added that, if the Council had certainty, or even hope, that the "Catholic princes from

---

[21] J. Rubsam, *Johann Baptista von Taxis, 1530–1610* (Freiburg-im-B., 1889).

[22] See also Stafford, pp. 239 ff.

[23] Maritime Museum (Greenwich) Philips MS. **91**, ff. 222–227, copy.

[24] E 2571/4 and 16.

[25] E 977 n.f. letter of 13 March, 1603.

abroad" would give sufficient help "they would easily be persuaded to exclude the Scot." Thomas Sackville insisted that the Council was well inclined to peace with Spain at the present, and that some of them regretted the behavior of their commissioners at the conference at Boulogne in 1600.[26] The Council of State already knew of James's peaceful accession when it considered the report from Sessa; it advised Philip that it was best "to keep the Catholics of England encouraged" but to do nothing else.[27] Undoubtedly the Council was mindful that Spain's finances were committed elsewhere, that Philip preferred peace with England, and that Henry IV and Clement VIII were certainly cool to the idea of Spanish intervention. Philip did not inform his envoy in Rome of this decision at once, nor did he indicate to Tassis the contents of Sackville's secret report but it does help to understand the presence of such optimistic letters to the English nobles in Tassis' portfolio.

Yet even as Juan de Tassis proceeded northward to Paris and Brussels new letters were reaching Rome from various English Catholics. These too began to be included in the Duke of Sessa's dispatches. The Superior of the English Jesuits, Father Henry Garnet, who had worked in secret among the English Catholics for nearly eighteen years, wrote on April 16 to Robert Persons in Rome that the accession of James had brought to the recusants "a golden time of unexpected freedom abroad." He found that many had a "great hope of toleration," as there had been "so general consent of Catholics" at James's accession. Garnet's warning seems to be aimed, unwittingly, at Sackville for he wrote that his English friends "were loath that any Catholic Prince or His Holiness, should stir against the peaceable possession of the kingdom." [28]

However, the reaction of the leaders of the English Catholics who were writing to Rome gradually became more anxious, than pleased, at King James's policy. A month later an urgent letter was sent to Cardinal Farnese, the "Protector" for England at the Papal Court, by the Archpriest Blackwell, who was the ecclesiastical superior of the English Catholic clergy. He appealed for diplomatic support from the Papacy lest King James would grow too harsh in his treatment of the Catholics. He warned that no toleration of recusants was intended and that the offensive oath of Supremacy was being rigorously required of all who would hold office under the new sovereign. He was particularly alarmed that a new order was being prepared which would expel all priests from England.[29] A copy of Blackwell's letter was given to the Spanish Ambassador to send to King Philip. Meanwhile, Father Robert Persons was receiving further reports from England. He informed the Duke of Sessa that several memorials had been presented to James stressing the loyalty of Catholics "in all temporal matters" but they were afraid that the new King would ask the Pope to suppress the English seminaries.[30] In Rome the impression had grown that James was now seeking a delayed revenge against the authors of the *Conference about the next Succession*. Sessa reported to the Spanish Council that Robert Persons and his circle were at the present "looked upon as lepers to be avoided by necessity." [31] Later Sessa noted, however, that there was considerable debate at the Papal court as to whether Clement VIII should urge all the Catholic princes of Europe, as Blackwell's letter had begged, to plead with King James that there should be "peace and alleviation for the Catholics." [32] The single merit that could be seen in the plan was that such continental pressures would possibly afford King James an excuse to allow some change.

After these unpromising developments, the doubts of the Duke of Sessa about the wisdom of Philip's policy become quite understandable. He advised the King in a dispatch of mid-August that later, after a treaty with England, something more beneficial to the Catholics might be obtained. He noted that a resident envoy could persuade James "to moderate the cruelty which he might wish to use against the Catholics." Probably Sessa was influenced by Father Persons who had offered the same advice to Don Baltazar de Zúñiga in 1601. As before, King Philip would not budge. In fact his reply actually reflected a cautious optimism. There was nothing to do at present, he advised, for he felt that things were not so well settled in England that they would not change.[33]

Apparently Philip's attitude was widespread at his court. Even a year later an English spy, Thomas Wilson, wrote to Robert Cecil that at a banquet in Valladolid he had observed that the nobles "fell on vantage what wonders they would do against England if peace did not take place, and founded their speeche upon the number of Catholics which were named to be 200 thousand, and upon the discord between English and Scots." [34] It may be worth noting here that a decade later the estimate of the Catholics had increased. Don Diego de Sarmiento reported to King Philip that recusants were roughly 300,000 and "schismatics" double that number.[35] The latter group was usually described as those who conformed occasionally under the fear of governmental coercion. From all of these reports it is clear that the Spanish court believed that there was a hard core of English Catholics of about

---

[26] E 977 n.f. "Los puntos de la Conferencia con el cauallero Tomas."

[27] E 1857/9 consulta of 17 June, 1603.

[28] Stonyhurst MS. Anglia III, f. 32.

[29] E 840/128.

[30] E 1857 n.f. consulta 31 July, on letters of 22 May.

[31] E 977 n.f. letter of 1 July 1603.

[32] E 977 n.f. letter of 15 July 1603; A.S.V. Fondo Borghese III 124g2 f. 29.

[33] E 840/266 and E 1857/243.

[34] P.R.O. S.P. 94/10/1 letter of April, 1604.

[35] *Documentos Inéditos* 4: pp. 70–78.

200,000 with a larger number of sympathizers, who were restless under the crown's policy, or who were *Politiques*. Obviously they were expected to be sympathetic to any efforts to achieve some measure of toleration.

The speculation at the courts of Valladolid, Brussels, and Rome about James's future policy towards the Catholics had recently veered to optimism through the recollection of some of the King's past statements. James had always insisted that he would be generous to anyone who was loyal to his title. Thus, when Henry Percy, the Protestant Earl of Northumberland, had assured James early in March, 1603, that he had questioned the Catholics of his household and was convinced that "all of them wish your Majesty the fruition of your right," James was effusive in his pledges. He had quickly informed Percy that he would not persecute "any that will be quiet and give but an outward obedience to the law." He did not, as yet, make it clear how the law would press on the consciences of recusants. Only a few months previously James had secretly written to Sir Robert Cecil about his concern that "great floods of Jesuits and priests dare both to resort and remain in England." He wanted the proclamation of November, 1602, banishing priests rigorously enforced: "blame me not for longing for the exemplary execution thereof, *ne sit lex mortua.*" [36]

Unfortunately during this very crucial early period the conduct of some Catholics did not encourage the King to become lenient. During his progress southward from Scotland to enter into his new inheritance, James had become very irritated at the conduct of an English priest named Hill. This foolish man had presented a petition to King James at York, during his brief stay there in mid-April 1603, "in the name of the Catholics of England." It is certain that Hill, who had led a dissolute life in Rome and in England, to which he had returned without ecclesiastical permission in 1599, had no authority from the Archpriest Blackwell who would not dare to approach the King publicly. It was the tone and argument of Hill's petition which were certain to arouse the worst suspicions of James. Hill compared the Catholics to the Israelites begging King Jeroboam for relief, and when none was granted, the ten tribes took the "just occasion to leave their due obedience." Then he argued:

If the chosen people of God . . . sought relief with such resolution as to leave their legitimate king, we trust that our deed can not be justly condemned as the Catholic subjects of your Majesty, . . . seek, in loyal submission, relief from their difficulties.

He went on to ask a full revocation of all the penal laws "by command of your Majesty." James ordered Hill arrested and brought to London where he remained in the Gatehouse by order of the Privy Council. He was indicted in the Star Chamber in April of the following year after being transferred to Newgate. [37]

It was evident that the Catholics would have to give a more intelligent presentation of their hopes and, if it were publicized, it would possibly counteract the blunders of Hill. This was to occur shortly after James's arrival in London. An anonymous petition signed simply "The Lay Catholics of England" was at once presented to King James and distributed elsewhere in the city. Its tone was suitably deferential in requesting only a moderate change in royal policy. It asked: "the free use of their religion . . . if not in publike churches at least in private houses, if not with approbation yet with toleration, without molestation." [38] It cited the example of King Henry IV's treatment of the Huguenots, but did not go so far, as it merely asked the suspension and not the revocation of the laws. The Catholic petition—or *Supplication* as it came to be called— provoked a bitter reaction on the part of certain Protestants who were apparently writing with royal approval. Early in May, 1603, Gabriel Powell, a young preacher at Oxford, published a lengthy three-part answer. He began by printing the full text of the Catholic *Supplication* and then wrote a parody of it to be read on the opposite pages. There followed a labored attempt to prove by "antecedent" and "consequence" that "Popery" was theologically false. The last section was a short essay listing fifteen reasons why Protestants could not tolerate Catholics. It asserted that Puritans and atheists were more to be trusted, and warned that toleration would only increase the Catholics' hope of a "full reestablishment" of their church.

A far more virulent attack on Catholics came from the pen of Christopher Muriell in his *Answer to the Catholiques Supplication*. He also reprinted the Catholic petition, but he annotated the text with a repeated assertion that "discord and rebellion are the chiefest virtues of your new false Catholike Romish religion." He was disturbed by the reference to Henry IV who was, he warned his reader: "surrounded by conspiring papists." [39] He forsaw dire troubles for the monarchy if Catholics were tolerated:

Did not a gracelesse monk poison king John? did not a cursed friar of France murder with a poysoned penknife the last disceased French King? did not Bishops, monkes, friars and Iesuits of Spayne cause the kings eldest son to be murdered in letting him blood?

Hardly had Muriell's book appeared when a substantial proof seemed to be at hand that his worst fears were correct. During June and July of 1603 there was the nightmarish attempt of two English priests, Watson and Clarke, who conspired with George Brooke,

---

[36] *Correspondence of James VI,* pp. 74–75 ; 31–32.

[37] The petition is in E 840/137. See also T. G. Law, *The Archpriest Controversy,* 1: p. 5 ; 108 ; W.C.A. Series A, 1: f. 51 Levison deposition ; *H.M.C. Salisbury MS.* 15: p. 232 ; W. P. Baildon, *Les Reportes des Cases in Camera Stellata,* p. 168.

[38] Folger Library MS. Xd 332 f. 2, contemporary copy.

[39] *An Answer to the Catholiques Supplication,* Sig. B₂, B₄

the brother of Lord Cobham, to imprison the King in the Tower until he granted toleration. Brooke was the link with a more deadly conspiracy by which his brother would eventually drag down Sir Walter Raleigh. The "Catholic" plot was the "Treason of the Bye" and the Cobham plot the famous "Treason of the Maine" which was aiming "to kill the King and the cubs." Only the timely revelation to the Privy Council of the perilous nonsense of Watson and Clarke by a secular priest named Barnaby and the Jesuit, John Gerard, saved the cause of the Catholics from the revenge of King James, who publicly expressed his satisfaction at the loyal conduct of his Catholic subjects.

Anxious to make a further royal pacific gesture the King, as part of his coronation festivities late in July, allowed pardons to be given to all recusants who would sue for them. The indictments for recusancy, however, he allowed to continue but a considerable number of remissions for the fines were also made. The receipts of the exchequer for 1604 from recusancy were to be only £1,414, which was nearly £5,700 less than the preceding year.[40] Despite these partial concessions James maintained his threatening pronouncements against Catholics. In the dispatches from Brussels to Spain he was still described as particularly vehement against those who were "Jesuitised," or "Hispaniolated."[41] Yet King James was as misleading on the Spanish question as he was on the toleration issue, for he was eagerly awaiting news of the progress of the official Spanish envoy to greet him on his accession to the throne, even while he denounced anyone favorable to Spain.

The journey of Juan de Tassis northward had been slow. His visit to his uncle in Paris had been discouraging for there he had been informed that King James was intransigent in all religious matters.[42] When he came to Brussels in the last days of June he was clearly not ready to proceed to England. He needed more advice about both the new King and the English Catholics; moreover, his latest instructions from the Spanish court had not arrived. The Archduke's ministers were anxious to impress upon Juan de Tassis that they had far more experience in English affairs and that he would do well merely to follow their lead. The Spaniard was annoyed at this approach which he considered to arise from cowardice rather than prudence.

Thus the advice of the Archduke's council did not affect Tassis' opinions in the slightest. He was clearly reserving his judgment when, for example, the President of the privy Council, Jean Richardot—whom Tassis rather sarcastically dubbed the "oracle of affairs of state here"—told him that the matter of religion was completely unnegotiable, "and without hope of success

even if there are negotiations." The court at Brussels, Tassis concluded, did not have any hope for a peace that would be "in keeping with the prestige and reputation of Catholic Spain."[43]

Tassis' reaction illustrated how far the deterioration of friendship between Valladolid and Brussels had progressed. Jean Richardot was not unknown to the Spanish court. His uncle, François Richardot, the cultivated Bishop of Arras was a founder of the university at Douai where he had taught theology until his death in 1574. Several of the Bishop's students had been distinguished English refugees from Oxford. Moreover, Jean Richardot had been a close friend of the Duke of Parma who had warmly recommended him to Philip II. He had lengthy diplomatic experience, and he would be the only diplomat of the three powers who had been at Vervins and Boulogne prior to the London conference of the following year. His advice would have ordinarily carried more weight except for the coolness between the Archduke and King Philip at this time. Typically, Tassis complained that the Archduke was not as frank with him as he should have been. He had become suspicious when he had learned that the Count of Aremberg had already been sent to England as an envoy, although bland assurances were given by the Brussels Court that it was merely to offer congratulations. Later Tassis would report that Aremberg was "exceeding his instructions" in many ways. The Archduke Albert had explained that Aremberg's early departure for London was urgent "because England was close to the Low Countries and he must be solicitous of affairs there." Similarly, there was very little news given to Tassis concerning the work of the Archduke's perceptive envoy in Edinburgh, Scorza,[44] and what was really more to Tassis' disadvantage, the secret mission of Dr. Robert Taylor to the Catholics of England was not as yet revealed to him. When the report of this English Catholic lawyer, who was sent by the Archduke to England, was finally made known to him it was done in a very guarded way although the information was more immediately useful to him. Tassis had some reason to be displeased with his reception in the Low Countries thus far.

Then the unexpected took place. As a result of the Spanish envoy's various encounters with English Catholic exiles in Paris and Flanders a secret meeting was arranged on July 3, with a special messenger, from various unidentified English Catholics, whose name was Robert Spiller. Before his startling advice can be revealed, the extant biographical data about this relatively obscure man can be presented.

Robert Spiller was the son of Sir Henry Spiller of the Court of the Exchequer, and a member of a London family whose religion has been described in Arthur Wilson's memoir, after two years' residence in that

---

[40] See London Sessions Records for 1603–1604 in C.R.S. **34** (1934); E 840/119 "avisos de Londres" 19 June; F. C. Dietz, *Smith College Studies in History* **13** (1928).

[41] E 622/97.

[42] E 2557/2.

[43] E 840/109.

[44] E 840/110–118; Stafford, pp. 244 ff.

household, as "some of them absolute, and others of them church papists." The description would fit the category of recusant and "temporizer." Robert's mother was described by Wilson as "a great papist." Some of his family were known to be assisting Father Henry Garnet and other priests in London and one of them—perhaps Robert—became Garnet's "domestic" for a period. In 1606 Sir Thomas Edmondes reported from Brussels that a spy in the preceding year had seen Robert Spiller in the company of Guy Fawkes. Consequently, during the search for any of that famous conspirator's acquaintances, Spiller, who had returned later to England, had to go into hiding. However, his father Sir Henry Spiller later reported to Phelippes, the famous figure in English espionage, that Robert was "out of their fingers." [45] Edmondes' report should be questioned, as in the spring of 1605 Robert Spiller had become a close friend of the household of the Comte de Beaumont, the French Ambassador in England. In a letter to Beaumont written in Paris in March, 1605, Spiller related that he had been unwell and was going to convalesce in the French countryside for two months, but that if the search for Catholic recusants in England abated he would like to visit London for a short time after Easter. Spiller did actually return to England later where he appeared to have remained a recusant, for even in 1626 he is listed among "those refusing to come to church." [46]

In a special dispatch in cipher Juan de Tassis described his encounter with this young English recusant. He said that Spiller was trusted at the court of the Archduke, that he was recommended by "the Catholics and the Theatines" [47] and that at one time he had been sending information to the youthful Spanish naval commander Federico Spinola—younger brother of the famous Marquis Ambrosio—who had been killed recently in a naval battle off Walcheren Island. Spiller was accompanied to the meeting by Sir William Stanley, who was at the time a member of the Archduke's Council of War; by Hugh Owen, who was a Welsh Catholic conducting some of the Archduke's espionage in England; and by Father William Baldwin, who was the superior of the English Jesuits in the Low Countries. The four exiles came to Tassis' lodgings "at a late hour of the night to protect ourselves from certain spies." [48] Tassis took notes as the four Englishmen discussed conditions in England, the atmosphere at James' court, and "what reliance the king places on certain people." Furthermore, there was abundant advice on a subject dear to the heart of any ambassador: what courtiers could be trusted when they promised to do something.

In the course of the night a list of names was drawn up which Tassis sent at once to Spain in cipher. [49] It gave first a characterization of thirteen members of the Privy Council, who had also served during the reign of Queen Elizabeth, and then turned to the seven new English members and five new Scottish additions. It closed with advice on various other influential court personages.

This report of Tassis has an unusual importance, but within certain obvious limits; it can provide some clue as to what, if any, was the degree of sympathy for toleration of Catholicism within the English Court; it also gives some understanding of the earliest phase of that alignment of courtiers who were, years later, to be described as a "Spanish faction." Above all, its immediate value is that it offers an opportunity to see upon what sort of information Tassis had to rely during the first months of his stay in England. As will be seen, he would eventually alter several of these characterizations in the light of his own experience, when he would draw up his lists for pensions on June, 1604, for the approval of the Constable of Castile. In the only copy available—a decipher in Spanish—the document retains its cryptic style of being notes on the conversations of that evening; there is a direct remark that more was to be told the envoy later: "the manner of winning over some of the Councilors will be declared by word of mouth and in more detail in England." There was also a warning that Tassis would have to always be on the alert, for "divers persons may attempt to insert themselves into your favor under pretence of being a Catholic or some other ruse." Tassis was instructed to give prior notice of any such approach to Spiller, or some other confidant, to avoid dangerous mistakes.

The list made it clear that an important number of influential English courtiers were still cool to having peace with Spain. There was little hope, it warned, that the Archbishop of Canterbury, the Earl of Shrewsbury, Sir William Knollys, Sir John Stanhope, Sir John Popham, Lord Burghley or Lord Zouche would alter their anti-Catholic sentiments. Significantly—and surely reflecting a widespread English prejudice—James's Scottish favorites: Lennox, Mar, Elphinstone, Bruce and Hume were characterized as bitter Protestants who, however, could change their opinion if bribed.

The picture was not entirely pessimistic for several courtiers were believed to be of considerable assistance to Tassis' mission. Lord Buckhurst was said to be inclined to a peace with Spain and even to liberty of conscience; his son, Thomas Sackville, would probably help Tassis to approach his father. The Earl of Cumberland, who was friendly to the secret mission of Dr.

---

[45] Peck, *Desiderata Curiosa* (1735 ed.) Book xii, pp. 7 ff.; *H.M.C. Salisbury MS.* **17**: p. 611; **18**: p. 11; *CAL S.P. Dom 1603–1611*, p. 294.

[46] Bibliothèque Nationale, Fonds Français 15977 f. 376 (I am indebted to Dr. J. Bossy for this reference). Rushworth, *Historical Collections* **1**: p. 396.

[47] "Theatine" was used regularly, but not exclusively, by the Spanish court decipherer for "Jesuit."

[48] E 840/109.

[49] E 840/118.

Robert Taylor, Sir Henry Wotton and Lord Mountjoy were all said to be well inclined to Catholics. William Howard of Naworth Castle—the younger brother of the powerful Earl of Suffolk—was known to be a Catholic but he rarely went to court. His importance would be only in possibly influencing other members of the Howard family. Sir John Fortescue, who was in declining health, was felt to be a "Catholic in heart." The Earl of Worcester, however, although formerly a Catholic, was felt to be too anxious to keep his new political position to be of any real use.

Other courtiers had what appeared to be a more neutral position. Egerton, the Lord Chancellor, and the Earl of Northumberland, though Protestants, were believed inclined to make peace with Spain but they would follow first the King's lead in this respect. It was suggested that Lord Chandos would help with Egerton, and Northumberland's Catholic brother, Charles Percy, would be an intermediary with the latter. Thomas Howard, the Earl of Suffolk, had profited from the war, and had had at one time at least two ships engaged in privateering.[50] The report said he would not be favorable at once to peace with Spain, yet he would certainly change and follow the King's opinion. Suffolk's uncle, Henry Howard, the Earl of Northampton, was described as a very doubtful Catholic: "he is of inconstant mind, and not as straight as he might seem in his speech." He also was expected to follow the King's policy. The Earl of Nottingham, Charles Howard, the cousin of Suffolk and Northampton, had profited well from his office as Lord High Admiral and it was thought that he would be the more obdurate of all the Howards towards a peace. The known anti-Spanish position of Sir Robert Cecil, then Viscount Cranbourne, was very discouraging to Tassis as the Principal Secretary was aptly described as "having at present more access to the King in matters of government than any other Englishman."

Thus the coldness and evasions of the Archduke had been replaced by a clearer picture of the sentiments of the English court. The envoy had now an idea of the number and quality of those who opposed him and of those inclined to favor him. There was only a small group of courtiers who would be willing to try to mitigate the recusancy laws. It was easily the most informative report that Tassis had obtained until then, and it seemed to contain enough to persuade the King of Spain, that despite the skeptical outlook of the Archduke, a diplomatic effort to assist the Catholics should be continued.

Hardly had Tassis dispatched the Spiller report to the Spanish Council of State, when there arrived in Brussels a person who fitted the recent warning of his friends about "one who may attempt to insert himself into his favor under pretence of being a Catholic, or some other ruse." This stranger only visited the Archduke Albert; he did not go near Juan de Tassis, who only learned of him by hearsay at the court. The ruse used by this new visitor was to pretend to carry a written report of what he claimed to be a meeting between Dr. Robert Taylor—the Archduke's envoy to the English Catholics—the Archpriest Blackwell and Father Henry Garnet. The visitor retained his anonymity since even the Archduke's special report of July 4 described him vaguely as "a very intelligent man who has been corresponding in England with the Fathers of the Society [of Jesus] in matters of religion."[51] The fact that he retained a hazy identity is hardly the primary cause for suspicion; what identifies him as a troublemaker in the prospects for peace was that his report contradicts all of Blackwell's and Garnet's authentic correspondence of this time. Besides, there was no need to deliver a written report from Taylor since that envoy had already left England on June 30 and was expected in Brussels at any day. There was even less need and greater foolishness in the dangerous expedient of putting in writing confidential remarks which Taylor was to relate very shortly. Furthermore, this unknown visitor's report is different in certain essential respects from the actual message that Taylor would bring.

The English Catholics, this self-styled messenger reported wildly, had no hope of getting the laws against recusants annulled, or of obtaining any form of toleration. He therefore advised the preparation for war saying that there was no greater opportunity for rebellion than the present as the English treasury was empty. This messenger had intimate knowledge of other self-styled envoys to Spain of equally dangerous intentions for he argued: "Some months before the Queen died, the English Catholics sent to Spain two people to present to his Majesty the miseries they suffered. They wished to show how ready they were to assist any design to reduce that kingdom to the Catholic faith." The envoy then informed the Archduke that they had prepared arms and horses and that their "party" had increased to 30,000 men and that 8,000 were ready "under arms." A provocative message indeed.

Since Juan de Tassis did not meet this Englishman he could only briefly report the news two days after the Archduke's dispatch was sent to Spain. Then he merely stated that a "confidant" of the English Catholics and the "theatines" had said that the Catholics were strong and could gather 12,000 men "under arms." The report had grown in being passed to Tassis by 4,000 men! "If it is true the advice is important," he commented, "and it demands deep consideration." But he was clearly thinking along other lines for he had become more interested in another report at the court which he suggested "would be more practical and easy if it is true." He had heard that "should your Majesty spend on the English and Scottish officials of that Court

50 *Hakluyt Society Series II,* 111 (1959) : p. 18.

51 E 622/96 and 97.

up to 500 or 600 thousand ducats, it will be possible to bring the king to the point of liberty of conscience." [52] Tassis implied that the matter should be probed.

Thus in one week Tassis had his first taste of the difficulties of trying to negotiate about English Catholic affairs. He had been told of the greed of English courtiers, of the anxious desire for peace of the Catholics, and of their supposed desire for war, and finally, of the refusal of King James to alter the laws. It was sufficient to make him despair of getting the truth about the situation, and his bewilderment was to increase. A week later on July 13 he wrote to Philip that the Nuncio in Brussels, Ottavio Frangipani, had been visited by someone posing as an "English theatine." This otherwise unidentified person was said to be *en route* to Rome to ask for papal military support for the candidacy of the Duke of Parma for the throne of England.[53] The known policy of Clement VIII in which the English Catholics were encouraged to submit to James peacefully was being deliberately ignored. This troublemaker had increased the armed forces of the Catholics to "more than 30,000 men." Tassis dutifully reported the message but without any special comment.[54]

Ultimately little harm was done by the false reports of the two messengers, as Tassis was a cautious man still waiting to learn more details of the problems of his mission in the relative safety of the Low Countries. Desperate schemes, bogus identities, lies, propaganda, and cynicism were to be the normal hazards of his embassy. He seems to have weathered his first experience well.

---

[52] E 840/119.

[53] E 840/173.

[54] In his dispatch Tassis said that he did not know the name of the Nuncio's informant, and wondered "if he is that same confidant as before who did not give his name," referring to the messenger who had falsified Taylor's reports. It is possible that Tassis had come into one of the many phases in the bitter vendetta of the Appellants with Father Robert Persons. One of the figures on the fringe of the Appellant clique was an ex-Jesuit lay brother named John Baptist Dorkins, who was dismissed from the Order in 1598. He had traveled to Rome and eventually secured ordination through forged credentials. He then moved to Flanders where he was imprisoned in 1601 (*Frangipani Correspondence* vol. iii/1 p. 249) for anti-Spanish agitation. Although he was released and expelled from the Spanish Low Countries he returned to Flanders at this time [posing as a "theatine"] and agitating for the candidacy of the Duke of Parma (*ibid.*, p. 858, the name is misspelt "Dochymum"). In announcing that some Catholics favored Parma, it would be easy for the Appellants, and one of their leaders, Father John Cecil, to protest Catholic loyalty to James and thus secure the King's favor (W.C.A., Series A, vol. vi f. 93, English Relation of John Cecil). Cardinal Aldobrandino, the Papal Secretary of State was deeply disturbed at this fraud, and an English agent of Sir Robert Cecil concluded from an intercepted dispatch: "Cecil the priest hath made a very false information of the Cardinal's treating with him to set up the Duke of Parma as king of England" (*H.M.C. Salisbury MS.* 15: p. 250). The subsequent activity of Aldobrandino to stop the fraud can be traced in his letters to the nuncios in Paris and Brussels in the *Frangipani Correspondence* 3(2): pp. 698 ff.

Meanwhile Doctor Robert Taylor had returned to the Low Countries and reported personally to the Archduke, but not all was told to the Spanish envoy. Since the message he brought was even more significant than Robert Spiller's, it will be useful to review this Englishman's career as well. Robert Taylor was born in Yorkshire but had left England early in the reign of Elizabeth. He studied Canon Law at the University at Douai where since early in the 1570's he had been lecturing. He finally came to the notice of the papal Nuncio, Ottavio Frangipani, who had sent him as an observer at the peace conference at Boulogne, where he penned nine short but accurate reports. Returning to Douai he was made *Doctor Utriusque Juris* in November, 1602, and in May of the following year he went secretely to England to observe Catholic affairs. At this time he was a pensioner of the Archduke for 30 escudos a month.[55]

The originals of Taylor's reports do not survive. Instead there are three different Spanish summaries: two were made from the decoded dispatches sent by the Archduke, and the third was a more general report prepared by Tassis. The first is a summary of what Taylor learned in his stay in England. The second is a very significant report of what precisely Taylor informed his friends in England about the present intentions of the Archduke during the coming peace discussions.[56] It is also a record of their reaction to his statement of the peaceful intentions of the court at Brussels.

The only explanation for this second report would appear to be to set the record straight after the disturbing false letter of the unknown "messenger" a few days before. The third Spanish report is merely the general summary of the situation which Tassis was given later. The Archduke reserved for himself the petty triumph of the precise names and places which he sent on to the Spanish court. Without the clarifying dispatch of the Archduke in some places, Tassis' account is misleading. For example, Taylor had an interview with the Earl of Cumberland, while Tassis only knew that it was "with the noble who will be named in time." [57] There must have been considerable mutual dislike to provoke such clumsy gestures which were ultimately to be to the loss of the Archduke, since the Council of State in Spain had already determined that the opinions of Tassis were to be awaited in all matters before Spain would approve of the terms for English negotiations.[58]

The most interesting part of Taylor's report concerned his conversation with the Earl of Cumberland to whom he was introduced by one of the Earl's broth-

---

[55] *Frangipani Correspondence,* 3(2): pp. 775–781; E 840/118.

[56] E 622/84, "Relación del Roberto Taylero de lo que se ha tratado en Inglaterra"; E 622/83, "La Relación que en Inglaterra ha dado el D. R. Taylero."

[57] E 840/178.

[58] E 2557/2.

ers. The Earl told Taylor that he was willing to do what he could in the matter of peace and toleration for Catholics, but "when the greater part of the Council votes for war he must stay with them."

During his secret journey to England, Taylor had as friend and adviser a man named Anthony Skinner, who apparently served as intermediary with other members of the English Court. How Skinner had an entree to such notables was never made clear; possibly, he was related to Alderman Skinner who was Lord Mayor of London in 1596 although that family did not mingle with recusants. It is certain that Skinner had formerly lived for some years as a servant of Cardinal Allen, later he had sought to enter the Society of Jesus but was not accepted. He had remained on the continent and traveled to Spain in 1589 where he served in the navy until he obtained an order from Philip II to the Duke of Parma in July, 1591, sending him to the forces in Flanders, "as the sea was not good for his health." Although he was given a good pension of 40 escudos a month he did not linger in the Low Countries but returned to London, as he claimed to have an income of 3,000 escudos—roughly £750—a year.

Shortly after his return Skinner was arrested and imprisoned in the spring of 1592. He was tortured into confessing a part in a plot to murder the Queen but he later denied any complicity. The news letters of Richard Versteghen reported his trial in London in August, 1592. At its conclusion he was condemned to death but—as an indication of his family's connections—"some kynde offer of pardon hath bene made to some of his friends for the some of 500 poundes." Sir Thomas Heneage was instrumental in saving his life. It is not known how long Skinner stayed in prison, but while he was there he had clearly earned the confidence of a very capable English spy, named William Sterrell, who asked on three occasions that Skinner be sent to Liege to confer with him.[59]

It is extremely likely that sometime in the 1590's Skinner became a spy and possibly even an apostate Catholic. His activities must have been very limited, since later on Dr. Robert Taylor and other leading English exiles never suspected him. It was through Skinner that Taylor was introduced to the Countess of Suffolk and Sir Thomas Lake. Little is known of Skinner's subsequent activities except that he was well protected at court, for at the height of the anti-Catholic furore in 1606 Skinner was able to obtain a license "to go to any parts beyond the seas and return without molestation."[60]

Through the efforts of Skinner, Taylor had a useful conversation with the Countess of Suffolk. He handed her a written statement showing the details of a plan for liberty of conscience, which unfortunately was not included in the dispatch of the Archduke. However, some idea may still be obtained from his notes on the reply of the Countess of Suffolk. She asked him whether the Catholics would be satisfied with having "Mass in their houses," and Taylor had replied—without any authority —that they would be. Tassis, as we shall see, thought at this time that this was an inadequate concession.[61] The Countess had then informed Taylor—without any real authority either—that, in return for written assurances of 200,000 escudos which were to be redeemed after the conclusion of "the peace treaty and the revocation of the penal laws," certain members of the Council, whom she did not name, would be favorable to the Spanish requests.

A few days later, again through the help of Skinner, Taylor had an interview with Sir Thomas Lake, who was King James' secretary of the Latin tongue and in favor with both the Scottish nobles and the Howards. Lake told Taylor that the Council was divided into three factions: a minority wanting peace, a second group wanting war "but their mouths could be stopped with money," and a third which would want war for they were already pensioners of the Dutch. Taylor gave to Lake the same written statement that he had earlier handed to the Countess. After an interval of five days, Lake informed Taylor that £40,000—a sum a little less than that mentioned by the Countess—would influence sufficient councilors to make peace. On the Catholic question Lake was more cautious, for he remarked that the Council would be willing to proceed "little by little" afterwards. Taylor then asked to have a visit with "the person who could do so much with the King," which was an obvious reference to Robert Cecil. To this Lake replied that Taylor should first return with the promises for money in writing before this favor was granted.

Each of the Spanish copies of Taylor's report, whether from the Archduke or in the summary form of Tassis, then concluded with an insertion of a statement said to come from Henry Garnet. It is only a summary of the report of the earlier unknown messenger who had preceded Taylor. According to this version the Superior of the Jesuits had urged Taylor to inform the Archduke that there never was a time more auspicious than the present "to reform the kingdom" by warfare.[62] The advice took on importance largely from the position of Garnet whose successful ministry among the recusants was well known. However, it contradicts Garnet's actual correspondence. In a letter sent to Rome at the very time of Taylor's visit to England, Garnet was extremely anxious over the rumors of discontent that were to be climaxed by Watson's notorious "Bye Plot." He was dismayed at the certain renewal of the persecution it would provoke. On June 15, 1603, he

[59] A.R.S.J. Anglia 38–II f. 78, Persons to Creswell (ca. 1589); A.H.N. Sección de Estado, lib. 251, order to Parma; E 622/84; C.R.S. 52: p. 57; CAL.S.P. Dom. 1591–1594, pp. 217, 225, 229.

[60] Cal. S.P. Dom. Add. 1580–1625, p. 486.

[61] E 840/173.

[62] E 622/224. Also Lonchay & Cuvelier, 1: p. 164, n. 1.

informed Robert Persons that the conspiracy of "discontented priests and laymen" had led the Archpriest to forbid strictly all his priests to take part in any such attempts. He commented bluntly: "It is nothing but a piece of impudent folly, for we know that it is by peaceful means that his Holiness and other princes are prepared to help us."[63]

Fortunately, what could have been a dangerous misconception over war and peace in the advice of the English Catholics was not believed by Juan de Tassis. Moreover, Dr. Taylor and Anthony Skinner stayed very briefly in Brussels and returned at once to England[64] to renew their discussions with their friends on the Council. It is certain, however, that Taylor did not bring back any promises about money since the Council of State in Spain had not as yet voted on the question. Taylor's usefulness to the Archduke was largely for information, since any discussion of payments to the English courtiers meant Spanish money. It is important, therefore, to understand how the Council of Philip III reacted to the information sent from Brussels during these early weeks of Tassis' journey northward.

The Spanish Court was residing in Valladolid at this time and it was there that King Philip convened his Council of State, which held three sessions in the last week of July, 1603. These meetings dealt almost exclusively with possible terms for a peace with England and in particular with the question of the English Catholics. It was clear that the Council—despite the misleading rumors relayed by Tassis and others—did not expect the peaceful accession of James to be challenged. The secret discussion with Robert Spiller and the reports of Doctor Taylor—although some of the council suspected the latter to be a fraud—had emphasized that money, either as open gifts or secret bribes, would assist all of the Spanish objectives. There was another reason for the distrust of Taylor which gives an insight into the attitude of the Council: they felt that Taylor was too timid in seeking only private worship for the English Catholics. It appeared that Taylor was only viewed as a partisan of the policy of the Archduke, who was hoping to end the war with the Dutch immediately, and to secure the English withdrawal from the cautionary towns in the North. The Archduke had decided that the Catholic problem had become the sole concern of Spain.

The Council of State was the major administrative body of the Spanish Hapsburg monarchy, along with the Council of the Indies and the Council of Finance. At this time its full membership was confined to fifteen nobles but it rarely assembled in plenary form. The debates on English affairs to be reviewed here were attended usually by six members, but these included the most influential voices at the Spanish Court. Juan de Idiaquez, the *Commendador Mayor de Leon,* was from a Basque family which had risen to serve in the lucrative posts of court secretaries to three generations of Hapsburgs. The great position of trust which Idiaquez shared with Cristobal de Moura during the latter part of the reign of Philip II had inevitably been diminished in the new atmosphere of the court of Philip III. Since Idiaquez had handled reports on England for nearly two decades he was the first to speak on the subject on this occasion. The Duke of Lerma had not as yet reached his full ascendancy as the favorite of the King, but his opinion was important since he inclined to peace.

Juan Fernandez de Velasco, the Constable of Castile, will be important because he was eventually to be Philip's official envoy at the signing of the peace treaty with England a year later. The Count of Olivares, who had served in Rome as Spanish ambassador for ten years from 1582 onwards, was well informed about English affairs. When Bastoni, the secretary to Camillo Caetani, the Papal Nuncio in Spain, reported four years previously on the Council of State he found the Constable and Olivares "hard and implacable men"; they had not changed in the interim.[65]

The Spanish Council had other reports to consider in judging the best policy to pursue in England. On July 13, 1603, the Duke of Lerma had handed to Philip III a translation of a *breve* from Clement VIII that urged him to make a permanent peace. In the crisis with England there were but two paths, wrote the Pope, one of peace and negotiation, and the other of violence which had produced nothing but misfortune in the past. Clement expressed his fear that without peace there would follow the destruction "of those few remaining Catholics in England"; he agreed to approve all that Philip would succeed in obtaining in his negotiations.[66] Philip decided to delay his reply to Rome until there was further word from his envoy in Brussels, but, even when he did so, he appeared to be afraid that Spain would appear weak to the courts of Europe if he was too conciliatory. He wrote to Sessa on August 23 that the Pope's letters "found me more inclined to the way of arms . . . for these delays can only serve to give time to let that king be established in his realm and thus to persecute the Catholics with more resource." He observed, however, that he would try and negotiate as long as it was useful and that the Duke of Sessa

---

[63] A.R.S.J. Anglia 38–II f. 172 v; His insistence continued in the letters of July and August (*ibid.*) minute of letter of July 6: "optat ut Papa aut Protector scribat ad omnes Catholicos ut quiete et pacifice se gerant . . ."; letter of 13 August: "Rogat ut pontifex prohibeat omnem vim, quam omnino futuram esse putat. . . ." In another of the same date: "Rogat ut Clemens furorem reprimat si possibile est. . . ." The Spanish Ambassador in Rome thought that the problem was so serious that he sent a special dispatch to Philip III telling him that the Pope was being urged to check any outburst among the Catholics "porque al presente no se vea, de ninguna parte, pudiessen ser socorridos y amparados de manera que alterarse" (E 977 n.f.).

[64] *Frangipani Correspondence* 3(2): p. 414.

[65] Hinojosa, *La Diplomacia Pontificia,* pp. 401–402.
[66] E 622/83.

would inform the Papacy of further changes.[67] Whatever the outward appearances that Philip was careful to preserve in Rome, in the consultations in Valladolid the Council was inclined to negotiate a peace. All the letters from every source were now given a thorough appraisal; their three *consultas*—the synopsis of their opinions—came to nearly ninety pages.

In the three-page opinion of Juan de Idiaquez it was evident that not merely were the peace negotiations to be pushed, but that money was to be voted as soon as possible. He devoted himself largely to planning how precisely this money could be used. He warned that the Spanish ambassador could hardly approach King James in person because of the loss of prestige from such a gesture. Yet the money must be offered in such a way that Spain "is rewarded in the effect"; the payments should continue only as long as "the effect" continued. Idiaquez advised that a sum of 200,000 escudos should be authorized at once. The Duke of Lerma was also inclined to authorize the money, he had another reason to support the scheme: should James' policy stir up the discontented Catholics, Tassis would have money on hand "and what is impossible now may become easy later." [68] He was obviously hoping that James would be forced to change his policy by some turn of events in England.

The rest of the Council was far less sanguine. The Count of Miranda did not object to authorizing the money, but he did not agree that liberty of conscience would come by such payments since there were too many opportunities for evasion. The Constable of Castile was very skeptical that there would ever be any satisfaction by money. The Count of Olivares was equally unsure of any results, he was inclined to authorize the money only because a temporary change in the lot of the Catholics made the expense worth while. Both Olivares and the Constable foresaw that any Spanish request for toleration for the English Catholics and the consequent freedom for many exiles to return would be countered by an English request for freedom for Protestants in the Low Countries and even in Spain. Olivares suggested that the Spanish could promise it when the Dutch "were truly obedient to their king." The Constable said merely that the question would have to be looked into further. He implied that Spain did not have an adequate counter proposal at the moment.

In another meeting two days later the basic policy that had been outlined by Idiaquez came under a courteous but rather serious attack by the Constable of Castile. He noted that the affair of the English Catholics was the gravest matter that could be presented to the Council and that it ought to make its policy more carefully so that a good beginning could be made. He urged more prudent deliberation. "Since the English are intelligent

and astute," he warned, "it is to be feared than Don Juan de Tassis, while having many good qualities, could be dismissed as a man who has not handled these affairs before." The King of Spain, he remarked, usually employed three or more of the most intelligent in his service in these matters. He noted the different objectives that the Archduke and Richardot were pursuing in the same preliminary negotiations, and therefore great caution was important in the final appointment of the Spanish ambassador. The Constable was obviously hinting that he should receive that post, and later in the autumn he would succeed.

As a result of the debates the Council was virtually agreed that there was no other course but to negotiate; the time had come for Philip III to give his own judgment. In his own hand on the margin of the first four pages of the *consulta* of July 26, 1603, Philip ordered that Tassis was to be instructed "to insist strongly on the liberty of conscience for Catholics which is what I desire the most. Tell him that there is to be no thought of the money as long as he succeeds in it and gets the assurances that he is to have it. To all those who have a hand with that King let a pension be offered each year according to their quality. This is to be for the years that they grant liberty of conscience to the Catholics." He also urged Tassis to work earnestly for the ending of the war with the Dutch and the return of the cautionary towns. "His final powers are to be drawn up in great secrecy so that they can be sent when it is convenient and at the same time I will decide on what other persons are to go." [69]

The rest of the period of Tassis' embassy was to be a valiant if unsuccessful attempt to carry out the policy formulated in Valladolid. While Tassis still waited in the Low Countries for fuller instructions, he received some new information on the activities of Dr. Taylor after his return to England to consult the friends of the Countess of Suffolk.

There is only one report surviving on this Englishman's second mission and as before it is not directly by Taylor himself. This time there is only a Spanish translation of a summary by Father Henry Garnet of what he had learned from Taylor in a secret meeting. Apparently some time in August, 1603, Taylor was interviewed by five members of the Privy Council, but the report of Garnet only concentrates on what interested him the most: a possible toleration for Catholics. What other points were raised cannot as yet be discovered. Unfortunately, Taylor and his companion, Skinner, were put under oath not to reveal the identities of the councilors.

According to this document, Taylor proposed that the question of toleration for the Catholics should be entrusted to the intervention of the Spanish ambassador with King James. When one of the councilors noted that this seemed to make some English into subjects of

[67] E 840/190–193.
[68] E 2513/102.

[69] E 2557/2.

the King of Spain, Taylor replied that it was not the intention of Philip to act as a sovereign but simply to assist the interests of Catholics. Turning to the problem of the recusancy laws the councilors suggested that they would be prepared to favor a return to the conditions established by the laws up to 1571, but that Parliament was in a different frame of mind and King James would never abandon any of his rights. They implied the repeal of all of the most onerous laws and fines, leaving always the statutes of supremacy and uniformity. According to Taylor, the councilors regretted that any religious matter should be considered treason. When the councilors came to name particular English Catholic exiles and inquire into their attitude towards a peace, Taylor reported that Father William Baldwin and Hugh Owen had been very active in urging negotiations, but there was general skepticism among these councilors as to the news.[70]

How genuine was this reported interview of Taylor? It is quite certain that Garnet did meet Taylor at this time for he refers to it in an authentic letter which contains certain phrases which also appear in this Spanish summary which has just been reviewed.[71] While such an interview could very well have taken place, to believe that five members of the Privy Council would sincerely favor such a drastic change in the recusancy laws surely invites skepticism. In effect, the interview can have had no other purpose than to be part of a campaign of the circle of the Countess of Suffolk to encourage the belief that some toleration could be granted. To obtain it, gifts and pensions, in which they would be the chief beneficiaries, were to be a primrose path.

Soon the usefulness of Taylor's unofficial discussions would decrease with the arrival of Tassis in England at the close of August. There is evidence, however, that Doctor Taylor remained secretly in England to advise the Spanish envoy for many months. At the end of the treaty conference Taylor was to return to Antwerp with a warm recommendation from Tassis to the Archduke for a larger pension.[72]

In the last weeks of Tassis' stay at the court in Brussels, Philip did not send any new instructions. At that time the King was again following closely the news from the Papal court. He was still disturbed that Clement VIII would not publicly endorse Spain's plans on behalf of the English Catholics. He was also annoyed at Henry's success in gaining rapidly an offensive alliance with England. In a dispatch of August 15 he advised Sessa what to say to the pontiff.

If through the obstinacy of the king [James] what we are seeking can not be obtained, His Holiness might reflect on what the office which God has given him obliges him to do for the honor of the church and the defense of the faithful. In this cause it would be as just to have a new crusade . . .

as it once was for the recovery of the holy places of Jerusalem. In such an event, as an obedient son, I offer all my resources . . . in support, and with the same determination as if war had returned.

He attacked Henry's recent alliance against Spain as unworthy of his title of "Most Christian King." Obviously he hoped that Clement would prod Henry into reversing his policy: "Perhaps through the words of the Pope, the Lord will move the King of France, yet in any case this effort will be valuable as a justification for what is intended in the future." [73]

Meanwhile, in Brussels the Archduke was restive over the delay of Juan de Tassis; he wrote rather frantically to Philip that King James was losing all interest in a peace. This was not true, but it was a sufficient excuse for pushing the envoy along the road to England. Thus, despite many forecasts of failure, Don Juan de Tassis embarked at Dunkirk on August 31 in the flagship of Sir Robert Maunsell, the Vice-Admiral of the Narrow Seas. The weather was fair and the reception on board ship most courteous. Late the same day he landed at Dover. One of the most far-reaching interventions in the history of Spanish diplomacy had begun.

III. FRIENDS AND ENEMIES, SEPTEMBER, 1603–MAY, 1604

The arrival in England of the ostentatious suite of the Spanish ambassador excited surprisingly little reaction. There were many reasons for this; the plague was particularly virulent in London and the court was moving about, and rarely in a sufficiently orderly state to hold a large public reception. Moreover, James was quite preoccupied with his own amusements and the hunting of the stag, so that he abandoned to an inner circle of courtiers the conduct of many urgent affairs of state. It was not taken to be a sign of hostility that Tassis had to wait over a month to present his credentials.

In any case the Spaniard needed the interval to learn more about conditions at court, and to prepare the reports on his personal reactions which were awaited in Valladolid. He had little difficulty in sharing the view of the Venetian envoy in London that James was deeply concerned over the religious tensions in his kingdom. He was also gratified when he received a letter from Philip III instructing him to continue his probe through his "confidants" of the court's attitude to toleration:

I order you anew to make greater efforts in this matter with suitable urgency at every opportunity. See to it that the Catholics have the public exercise of our holy faith. . . . Since everything has to proceed by money the plan is to win over by payments the favorite officials of the king.[1]

Philip was now acting alone. Sessa reported in exasperation that Clement VIII was under the impression

---

[70] E 622/224.

[71] Stonyhurst MS. Anglia 38 f. 186, Minute of letter of 26 August.

[72] E 841/118.

[73] E 191 n.f. letter of 15 August, 1603, copy.

[1] E 2557/3 and 4, letter of 23 Aug., 1603; Cal. S. P. Venetian 10: pp. 41, 102.

that the war between England and Spain might soon reopen. He related that the Pope had pleaded with him to use extreme care to prevent a breach of the peace, "unless the king of Spain is forced to wage war after that king has suggested insolent terms." From Brussels the Archduke wrote that Philip's project was simply a waste of time. "After the peace is concluded efforts to gain freedom of conscience can begin," he advised on September 8, "if this is placed on the agenda in the first instance, it will damage and alter the negotiations about every thing else." Even by the end of September the Council of State was also having some misgivings about Spain's chances. It noted quietly: "Although discussion has begun about what should be done in case the king of England will not grant any toleration of the Catholic religion," it would await the direct reports of Tassis.[2]

The first letters of the Spanish envoy showed a ready grasp of the English attitude towards the principal grievances about religion. His report omitted any new information about toleration; instead he stated simply that he had learned that the English were agitated about the practices of the Spanish Inquisition against merchants, and the activities of the English colleges at Valladolid and Seville.[3]

The absence of an active concern about the English Catholics among the Catholic princes had not gone unnoticed by King James. There were many rumors about a common league on the question, but nothing reliable had come to his ear. To sound out the attitudes of the Catholic courts in France and Italy, King James had dispatched Sir Anthony Standen in July with the task of spreading reports of James's benign attitude to Catholics, of dusting off the hints of his possible conversion. It was a bizarre mission in many respects, for the King was not seriously worried over Standen's failure to report. In October he styled him "a pretty messenger in sooth," but added, "at all events if he has executed my orders properly he will have nothing to report on his return, but what I have already imagined."[4]

Despite the calculated spreading of propaganda on the continent, James did not deviate from his policy at home of "maintaining religion" intact by requiring conformity to the law. However, he advised Archbishop Whitgift privately that he did not wish "the shedding of blood" over diversity of religion.[5]

Tassis was soon convinced that James was definitely intending to negotiate a peace treaty with Spain although he was notably silent on the Catholic question. The Spaniard consoled himself in his early weeks in England by listing all the rumored reasons why James felt this way. His memorandum, entitled "The reasons

why the King of England is inclined to peace," is in many ways a summary of all the gossip and speculation that Tassis had by then encountered. He wrote

The King is of a timorous character . . . he plans by this peace to give every Prince the conviction that their tranquility depends on his will . . . a rumour has reached Scotland that the Pope would unite both France and Spain not merely against the Turk but against England . . . the King feels indebted to Spain for the past. . . .[6]

During this time Tassis also found that his earlier suspicions against the Ambassador of the Archduke were being confirmed. In a dispatch composed at Oxford on September 14 he complained that Aremberg's secret activities far exceeded his known instructions. The source of his knowledge about his rival he revealed to be "two English Catholics" who came to see him "at the court of this king." One of them had spoken to him before at Brussels and was well recommended by the English exiles in Brussels "who were all in correspondence with those of this kingdom."[7] The description would fit the visit of Doctor Robert Taylor in the Low Countries seven weeks before, and the other "Catholic" could then be Anthony Skinner.

These two confidants gave further news of their meetings with some members of the Privy Council. One of them was Robert Cecil of whom Tassis wrote: "he is, and will be, a man of the greatest importance." The confidants reported that the councilors were willing "to agree to the Peace" on the payment of 600,000 ducats. They added that, if 200,000 ducats more were available, six more councilors would agree to the peace. The amount was very large for it was approximately £125,000. The term "peace" was not explained any further, but the message would have little meaning unless it meant one suitable to Spain. Otherwise the bribe would be merely for the conclusion of hostilities, something that James was intending to do anyway. The news of a peace possibly favorable to Spain was received by Tassis with an obvious reserve. He simply informed the two "confidants" that his instructions from Philip III were to seek friendship and peace with England but that he would have to see these courtiers first for it was easy to harm the planning of a peace by ignoring the details. He then gave his first offer: "if those who spoke of peace would serve us to the benefit of Christianity and the Catholics of England" he was prepared to offer honorable gifts.[8] This first exchange came to nothing, but the series of confidential exchanges had only begun; there were to be many more during the coming months, and Tassis obviously felt that it was better to wait. In the meanwhile, the activity of Aremberg was apparently becoming of less significance at the English Court. He had no money, nor was the

[2] E 1857/22; E 622/143; E 2557/6 consulta of 27 September, 1603.

[3] E 840/187.

[4] Cal. S.P. Venetian 10: p. 100; See L. Hicks, "The Embassy of Sir Anthony Standen," Recusant History 5 (1960) : 186 ff.

[5] Cal. S.P. Dom. 1603–1610, p. 41.

[6] E 840/256.

[7] E 841/141.

[8] E 841/141.

Archduke willing to authorize any attempt at bribery on his part.[9]

Obedient to Philip's special orders, Tassis added his first impressions of the urgent question of the Catholics. "What is doubted by everyone here," he wrote,

is that the King would come to permit the Catholic religion. He is making it a point of honor whether the world should see that your Majesty, by negotiations, could now set up a law and religion in this kingdom . . . while some are of the opinion that to be assured of the Catholic faction, the King would dissimulate to the point of not persecuting the Catholics, he will not allow them to practice their religion in their houses without external conformity.[10]

Tassis could easily imagine Philip's reaction to this report, for he began to describe the difficulties inherent in Spain's objectives. James, he explained, was a thorough Protestant, thereby pointing out the deception that Philip had been experiencing for over a year from James's emissaries. Moreover, at the English Court there was a common opinion that any toleration would require the return of Church property seized decades before. Significantly, Tassis added another observation that showed the difficulty of his position: very few English Catholics were coming to visit him. He wrote that at the time it was because of the fear created by the downfall of "certain nobles," although he gave no details.

Two weeks later he wrote from Southampton another summary of what he had learned since his arrival in the Low Countries three months before. He was evidently beginning to share somewhat the opinion of the Archduke that it was better to defer the matter of religion until after the treaty. Yet there was an obvious hesitation to make this change of policy too explicit. He observed that undoubtedly there were many places in England where mass was celebrated, "and not with such secrecy that the king does not hear of some of them and permit them." However, to improve on this situation a peace would have to be first concluded and a system of bribery established. In this way, he observed, the Spanish would only be imitating the Dutch and the French, who were already doing it. He begged Philip to send more explicit instructions on how much he would be allowed to offer in the matter of pensions. He hinted that they would have to be generous and he remarked—much as the Venetian and French ambassadors were reporting—that at the English Court "the people are greedy and shameless robbers."[11]

In the same dispatch Tassis decided to give his impression of the Catholicism of Queen Anne. Although he had not as yet seen her in an audience, a Scottish nobleman who had her confidence, had visited the Spanish envoy. It was Sir James Lindsey, brother of the Earl of Crawford, who had been an envoy to Pope Clement VIII late in 1602. Lindsey was certainly a devoted servant of James, and never as irresponsible as Anthony Standen, but his journeys to Rome would have the similar effect of leaving a false mirror of James's real intentions. In this visit to Tassis there is little doubt that Lindsey was acting under James' instructions, as he brought to him the credentials under the great seal, which he said he would soon bear to Rome on his second mission. Actually his departure was to be postponed by the King until late in 1604.[12]

Lindsey recounted to Tassis how, earlier in the year, he had brought letters from the Pope and Cardinal Aldobrandino to the King and Queen. Since the Duke of Sessa had already reported to the Spanish court on Lindsey's activities, the news was clearly meant to remind Tassis of the good report of James currently circulating in Rome. The Scotsman also spoke at length on the religious observance of Anne, describing her acquaintance with the Jesuit, Robert Abercrombie, in Scotland who gave her the sacraments before she journeyed to England. He mentioned the private oratory in her apartments where on one occasion when James entered she refused to speak to him but only "outside the door." What Lindsey hoped to gain by this interviw was not too clear. He suggested that Tassis should cultivate the patronage of the Queen by writing to her in French as she knew no Spanish. Tassis reflected and then declined to do so for the present. He felt certain that King James would intercept the letter.[13]

Finally Tassis' period of waiting was over; after two further brief postponements, James indicated that he was ready to receive the ambassador of Philip III. The minute report of the Venetian Ambassador is a much sounder guide to the events of October 8 than Tassis' own rather terse dispatch. It appeared that both sides were over sensitive to petty details. Tassis, who was obviously nervous, forgot to remove his hat until he was halfway into the audience chamber; King James on reading the formal letter of congratulations was irritated that Philip called him "relative" not "brother"; both parties spoke their native tongue through interpreters rather than using French which both handled competently. All in all, it was a tense ceremony with little sincere expression of amity on either side. For the moment there appeared to be wisdom in the contemporary remark of Robert Cecil that, while there would always be peace between Spain and Scotland, between Spain and England it was merely a case of enemies being reconciled.[14]

Three days later James granted a more satisfying private interview to the Spaniard. At this time he was presented with the special gifts sent by King Philip.

[9] E 2557/2 consulta on dispatches from Brussels.
[10] E 841/141.
[11] E 841/155.

[12] See Stafford, pp. 239–240; Cal. S.P. Venetian 10: p. 224; Gardiner, 1: pp. 224–226.
[13] E 841/155. See also Cal. S.P. Venetian 10: pp. 68 and 81
[14] Cal. S.P. Venetian 10: pp. 102 and 108.

There were spirited Spanish horses with which James was delighted and three splendid jewels for Queen Anne. At this time James made it clear that he was anxious for peace and visibly disappointed that Tassis had not been given the full powers to negotiate.[15] Actually Philip had conferred these full powers on the Constable of Castile on October 1, but the full reports of Tassis' reception were still being awaited in Spain. The Constable did not leave Valladolid until October 30.[16] The Constable was in no hurry; he was to take two months to reach Brussels and then he was to resort to further excuses for delay.

On October 12, shortly after his private interview with the King, Tassis again warned Philip in unequivocal terms: "In the matter of the free exercise of religion for the English Catholics I am of the opinion that it should be left aside until the peace has been negotiated."[17] But the matter had gone further than he suspected. The rumors of Spanish concern over the Catholics had grown stronger and had at once become linked with stories of Spanish gold being brought into England. It was soon reported by the Venetian ambassador that important English councilors were to be pensioned but no terms were known.[18] There was however an even livelier reaction which can be traced in the letters of some of the leaders of the Catholics in England. Father Henry Garnet, for example, wrote of the new hope that burned brightly that the princes of Europe would help to buy some measure of toleration. He had written on September 21 to Father Robert Persons in Rome: "I pray you solicite that they [the Spanish] will give money for any little ease, for that will bring on further benefits. If they will not give it all, methinks all Christian princes might concurre with the Pope."[19] Evidently during the first weeks of Tassis' journey to England some sort of plan for buying toleration had been discussed prematurely in Rome and had been rejected outright by Clement VIII. The papal objections were not that it was impractical, but rather that it was unworthy and scandalous to buy toleration of a belief that could come, by its own teaching, only from God's blessing.[20] This was true but irrelevant, since only a civic toleration was at issue.

But the most lively interest in the rumors was clearly displayed by the Countess of Suffolk. By October 23 the Spanish envoy had had several discussions with her as to his prospects. In a letter of that date he referred to her as "the person in whose hands lies all the affair of the bribes." He said that he had been told that the Dutch would not come to a peace conference unless Spain ordered the Archduke to grant them complete toleration in Flanders. Tassis had told her that toleration would have to be allowed in England as well as Holland so that an impasse had been reached for the moment. However, there was a more promising lead in another direction. There was talk of a marriage alliance to be planned between the young Infanta with Prince Henry. Tassis had told the Countess that there was no hope of success in that discussion unless it was preceded by many years of freedom for the Catholics.[21]

Thus Tassis was patiently proceeding to learn the obstacles in England to his project, yet still trying to find a way to gain support for a suitable peace treaty. However the rumors continued to run far ahead of his actual negotiations. On October 30 Henry Garnet wrote to Persons that before the opening of Parliament was the best chance to bribe the King and the Councilors so that all the laws against the recusants would be repealed. The incredible sum he suggested—one million ducats—was a risk and an extravagance that Spain would never contemplate. The urgent tone of his letter makes it clear that there was a lively hope for some arrangement. A month later Garnet was again urging Papal support for Spanish efforts. He observed that reliable promises of money were sufficient: "neither do they here ask money but only assurance 'till all be done, but we desyre haste."[21a]

But there could not be haste. James was still determined on reform and "outward conformity." In December, 1603, he had drafted an order to Archbishop Whitgift to require the enforcement of all laws,[22] but since many of the fines were apparently not exacted for the moment, the full sting of the penalties was not felt. After observing this policy in action, Tassis concluded that James truly peacefully inclined but "very weak hearted underneath."[23]

There was no reaction from Rome despite the urgent appeals from Father Garnet. Anthony Standen who had picked up garbled reports in Italy concerning these proposals to buy toleration—by the time he reported on it, the English Catholics were bribing Scottish nobles to influence King James—remarked that from Rome "no answer returneth but words."[24] Clement was clearly adhering to his policy of avoiding for the present the open discussion of toleration and merely cultivating James's friendly opinion of him. Even in the Spanish Council of State the voices that in July expressed misgivings about Philip's desire to insist on toleration as the first condition of peace were growing louder. In November the *consulta* on English affairs expressed a

[15] E 840/253 and E 840/181–183.

[16] P.E.A. reg. 364 f. 23–24 and testimonial of 2 May, 1604; *Relacion de la Yda del Condestable de Castilla* (Valladolid, 1604), p. 4.

[17] E 840/241.

[18] *Cal. S.P. Venetian* 10: p. 82, 104.

[19] Stonyhurst MS. Collectanea P f. 597.

[20] P.R.O. Roman Transcripts, 31/9 bundle 89, letter of Aldobrandino of 8 September, 1603.

[21] E 840/264–265.

[21a] A.R.S.J. Anglia 30–II f. 176 v; Stonyhurst MS. Collectanea P f. 596.

[22] *Cal. S.P. Dom. 1603–10* p. 60.

[23] E 840/265.

[24] *Cal. S.P. Dom. Add. 1580–1625,* p. 434; E 2557/6.

clear warning not to allow any interruption from any source in the negotiations for peace.

Philip, however, decided to let his original instructions to remain unaltered. Still, he did not show any impatience with the noticeable lack of agreement on the part of his envoy who began to devote the larger part of his dispatches to nonreligious affairs. Actually the King of Spain was quite satisfied with the patient work of Juan de Tassis; late in the autumn he conferred on him the title of Count of Villa Mediana.

It was during this apparent doldrum in the diplomatic negotiations between England and Spain, when neither side was energetically striving to get a conference underway, that Tassis had an opportunity to reconsider his position. Since toleration was still the first condition of peace the only possible means was to make some payment of money. Even when the money became available, to whom should it be given? How should it be done? What degree of toleration would be compatible with English and Spanish objectives?

The answers to these questions had to be carefully prepared. Tassis was certain that an approach should not be made to King James. He was cynical about James's frequent hints to Rome as to his own conversion, and he implied in his reference to James's timidity that he felt insecure in his new kingdom. There were enough precedents in the preceding decades of kings being subsidized and assisted by foreign princes. Henry VII and later Henry VIII had received yearly payments from France to ensure their friendship and keep them from forming harmful alliances from 1492 to 1512. Even in Scotland, King James had received an annual subsidy from Queen Elizabeth from the time of the treaty of Berwick to insure his neutrality. It would appear that the hesitancy of Tassis in approaching King James was based solely on his belief that James was too sensitive over the question of the Catholics. He turned to the leading courtiers instead. The idea had already been implicit in the advice of Robert Spiller in Brussels and had been furthered by the Countess of Suffolk. The Spaniard did not even seem to be aware that Philip II had promised during the reign of his wife Queen Mary to pay over twenty pensions to various courtiers as gifts or payments for services rendered.[25]

At this time Katherine Knyvet Howard, the wife of Thomas Lord Howard de Walden, the Earl of Suffolk, was only one of several ladies of the court who had an established role in doing favors, for which fees, perquisites, and even bribes were expected. Lady Edmondes, for example, had secured £1,000 from a single client for helping to obtain a request.[26] But the career of Lady Katherine Howard was to be outstanding in this period for her undisguised ambition for money and power. Fifteen years after this time she

and her husband were to be indicted for extortion, bribery, and the falsification of the inventories of the Crown jewels. The Earl and Countess of Suffolk were sent to the Tower from which they were later released. Even though Sir Francis Bacon was an enemy of the Howards there is a very authentic ring to his charge at the time of their prosecution: "that Lady keeping the shop and Sir John Binglie, her officer, crying: 'What do you lack?'"[27]

It is noteworthy that in her exchange of information with Tassis the Countess of Suffolk only offered a picture of England's objectives; she did not sacrifice any of England's public interests. However, Tassis' letters leave little doubt that she was a venal, grasping woman. In an undated dispatch, which was received in Spain shortly after Tassis was given his title of nobility, he summarized under six headings all of the news the Countess had given him during the autumn. Toleration was not discussed separately but always in its relation to politics in England.

In the first place he noted that England was determined to end the war and forget the past completely. Then he added a curious bit of information. He had been told that if Philip and the Archduke hoped to have an offensive and defensive league with England it would be necessary to join a common expedition to recover Calais. "As they believe it was the fault of your father," he explained to Philip III, "that it was lost and was the principal reason why England broke with the Hapsburgs."[28] It was a futile move, as the Calais question had been settled by Spain in France's favor at Vervins in 1598.

Secondly, Tassis was informed that the English Court felt that, since Spain could not attend to all of her realms in the new world, the prohibition of trade there was nothing but insolence. Furthermore, the activities of the Inquisition should at least be limited to offenses publicly committed in Spain. The Countess turned to the Catholic question in its relation to the Papacy. Any peace between countries, she warned, was according to custom always inclusive of the friendly allies of each country, yet "there will not be a peace between England and the Papacy." Tassis was told that, in the Pope's dispute with the King of England, he would probably force into action "those princes who recognise his power over their consciences." Obviously Clement's conciliatory attitude to King James was being discounted by the Countess' circle of friends. Tassis was told that the "difference in religion" would force "many" to leave England. The Countess was very outspoken against the English colleges in Spain. These, she asserted, were established "to set England on fire and sow dis-

[25] Cal. S.P. Spanish, 1555–1558, pp. 454–456.
[26] See J. E. Neale, Essays in Elizabethan History, pp. 65–66.

[27] Arthur Wilson, Complete History of England (1706 ed.) 2: p. 705; see Joel Hurstfield, The Queen's Wards, pp. 180–188 for a discussion of court corruption at this time.
[28] E 840/140 "Relacion sacada de avisos dados al Conde de Villa Mediana por un confidente."

sension." She counseled Tassis that the students should be dismissed "as Philip II once agreed to do at the request of Queen Elizabeth," in a reference to the migration of the English students from Douai to Rheims.[29]

Concerning the United Provinces, Tassis was told that King James would not assist rebellion, but his English subjects would be angry if the money loaned to the Dutch were abandoned, and that the King's own inclination was to act as a neutral mediator.

Inevitably, the Countess of Suffolk could be expected to reach the subject of money. She startled Tassis by again urging the marriage alliance between the Prince of Wales and the young Infanta and observing that under the pretext of a partial payment of the dowry King James could be given a large sum of money "and thus Spain will break up all the schemes of the French, the Venetians, the Florentines and others." [30]

The character of the Countess was revealed quite clearly in these points. She was a greedy woman neither pro-Spanish nor pro-Catholic, but was—as Tassis would later shrewdly remark—a *politique*. The value of her advice was that it revealed to Tassis why a treaty of peace was not imminent; both sides would have to abandon cherished objectives.

In Spain the attitude of the Council of State continued to be critical of Philip's decision to insist on toleration. The Primate of Spain, Bernardo Cardinal de Rojas y Sandoval, who may be presumed to be sensitive to the problem of the English Catholics had by now aligned himself with the majority opinion. In a memorandum on the subject he observed that there were two motives for protecting Catholics outside the Spanish kingdoms, one from justice and one from charity. Justice, he warned, was obligatory only with those who were Philip's personal subjects. "The present case of the Catholics of England is one of charity and not of justice." [31] He advised that Philip had no obligation to exhaust Spain's resources and place everything in the greatest jeopardy: "Your Majesty is not obliged to break off negotiations for the point of conscience." In addition to the Church even the powerful Council of the Indies was in a conciliatory mood to England. In October, 1603, it ordered that all Englishmen taken prisoners in the Indies and now held in the *Casa* at Seville were to be released.[32]

As the storms of December, 1603, began to restrict the flow of correspondence between Tassis and the Spanish Court, the exchange of instructions began to diminish noticeably. There was very little traffic across the English Channel, for the Archduke reported to Philip that he had very slight news from the few Englishmen coming to Flanders at that time.[33] Tassis

apparently continued to cultivate the circle of the Countess of Suffolk, but the fact that he had limited powers for negotiation and that he was still concerned over toleration did not make his relations easy with King James. Obviously anxious to encourage the view that he was to be trusted in the question of the Catholics, James sent Sir James Lindsey again to Tassis to speak of the Catholicism of his wife Queen Anne. Once again the letters between Clement VIII and Anne were shown to the Spaniard who showed enough interest this time to send copies to Spain in cipher.

During December and January there was very little real progress in his mission. While staying with the court at Richmond, Tassis wrote on January 31 that as far as he could see the Catholics were a small and dispirited group who were careful to stay away from him. He did not see the obvious reason for this practice: that they would be observed doing so; instead, he appeared to be rather piqued:

During my stay in this kingdom, I have not seen nor has there entered my doors a Catholic of importance, nor do I believe that there are here those on whom a foundation could be made . . . no one speaks a word in favour of innovations and changes . . . no Jesuit has visited me nor has their Archpriest written to me except for two or three solitary letters about how they are suffering and the fears they have.[34]

Tassis was not to hear again from Spain until April. Communications were slow and Philip III was waiting for the reports of his new official commissioner for the treaty, the Constable of Castile. Juan Fernandez de Velasco, Duke of Frias and Constable of Castile had been staying for two months at the Archduke's court in Brussels. He was known to be ambitious to play an active role in the restoration of the Dutch provinces to Spanish control. He had long been a close friend of Baltazar de Zúñiga, the Spanish diplomat in Brussels who later was to be one of the chief figures—along with Bedmar in Venice and Gondomar in England— in an energetic Spanish diplomatic offensive in central Europe.

Reading the comments of the Constable in the Council of State prior to his journey northward one is impressed by his reluctance to further the pacific policies of Juan de Idiaquez and the Duke of Lerma. It is significant that he was given the assignment to England. He was not anti-English for, unlike Cecil, he did not consider England and Spain to be natural enemies. His interests, however, were similar to those of Zúñiga: the quest of Spanish power and prestige on the continent in the north. A treaty with England, therefore, must not diminish Spanish prestige. England must be a friend, but Spain's real interests were to be elsewhere. For him the English Catholic question was of no real importance, since Spain could not do very much about it unless it would divert far more of

[29] *Ibid. puntos* 2, 3, 4.
[30] *Ibid. puntos* 5 and 6.
[31] Lonchay and Cuvelier, 1: p. 175.
[32] E 840/249.
[33] E 623/3.

[34] E 842/154 and enclosures.

its resources from its more urgent objectives on the continent. This he apparently would not allow.

The Constable had reached the Low Countries early in January. It was soon evident that he had no intention of hurrying to England. He even informed Tassis that he preferred not to cross the Channel but to hold the peace conference in some neutral site. King James was furious when he learned of this; Spain had sent one envoy without full powers, and now another was across the channel without any wish to come to England at all. For three months, to James' annoyance and the increasing interest of those who opposed the peace in England, the Constable refused under various pretexts to leave the Low Countries. He complained of the gout, he hinted at problems of precedence arising from the earlier arrival of Tassis in England, he announced that he required further advice from the King of Spain.[35] Writing to Philip late in February he made clear the real reasons for his behavior. They were consistent with his opinions revealed earlier in Spain.

If I were in England, [he wrote,] it would show an excessive desire for agreement and therefore a loss of reputation. Thus success in these negotiations would be doubtful . . . on the other hand we now have greater hopes to succeed in what is desired, as there is a negotiation going on with those lords who most incline to peace.[36]

The Council of State endorsed the Constable's policy of awaiting a more auspicious time before moving to England.

Events were to take another turn, but for the worse, and in a direction which had been foreseen in the anxious letter of the Archpriest soon after James' accession. On February 22, 1604, King James issued a proclamation ordering all priests to leave England. It was, in fact, merely a renewal of Queen Elizabeth's order of November 5, 1602, which James at that time had secretly endorsed. Ironically the new severity was justified according to James by the "late conspiracy." A reference undoubtedly to the "Bye Plot" of the preceding summer, although James had then approved of the actions of the Catholic clergy in reporting it.[37]

The motives for James' harsh policy at this time must not be sought in "conspiracy." With Parliament about to convene in four weeks he did not wish the critical Puritan faction in the Commons to accuse him of official laxity. The English Catholics at once published another petition to the King.

From one of the secret recusant presses in London John Colleton's *Supplication to the Kinges most Excellent Maiestie Wherein several reasons of State and Religion are Briefly Touched* appeared as a memorial "to be read and pondered by the Lords, Knights and Burgesses of the Present Parliament." It defended the Catholic body "as not inferior to the Protestant or Puritan either in number, alliance or generositie of spirit and resolution." It begged the King to "reverse" the penal laws and allow Catholic worship in private; it did not demand public worship in churches. It cited the toleration practiced in other parts of Europe: "Germany, France and Poland and other countries where diversitie of religion is licensed by supreme authority, and the like have found peace wrought and established thereby. . . ." It recalled the Protestant pleas in England for liberty of conscience in the past and observed

the favour we sue for is but the benefit of that position which they held for most true and scripturall so that if they should now depart from that doctrine they must needs give the world to see that either then they did wittingly maintain the position against truth . . . or generally erred in that poynt of doctrine . . . which breathing clemencie did most recommend and give greatest increase to their religion.[38]

The work created a stir in London not merely because of the inevitable notoriety attached to a secret publication, but because of its timing to meet the opening session of Parliament. Two works were soon licensed which defended the Crown's policy. The first was *The Supplication of Certaine Masse Priests falsely called Catholikes* which was a hasty reprint of Colleton's book with a rather scurrilous gloss in the margin answering the "libeller's reasons." The second was another earnest effort by the industrious, if unconvincing, Gabriel Powell of Oxford. His *Consideration of the Papists Reasons of State and Religion for Toleration of Poperie in England* never approached the point that Colleton had made in his request for a civic toleration. Powell's oft-repeated theme was that James could not tolerate blasphemy, and thus "poperie" was out of the question.

Stimulated in part by this theological debate, James decided to place in his speech at the opening of Parliament a statement in which he hoped to placate the Protestants, and still offer some hope to the Catholics. On March 19 he explained to the assembled Houses that he did not wish to persecute the Catholics or "practice the thralling of my subjects in matters of conscience." He asked the members of Parliament whether they considered the present recusant laws satisfactory:

Even now at this time, have I been careful to revise and consider deeply upon the Laws made against them [the Catholics], that some Overture may be proposed to the Present Parliament for clearing these laws by Reason . . . in case they have been in times past further or more rigorously extended by Judges than the meaning of the Law was, or might tend to the hurt as well as of the innocent as of guilty persons.[39]

[35] *Cal. S.P. Venetian* 10: p. 130, 133; *Lettres de Cardinal d'Ossat* 5: p. 269, n. 2.

[36] E 2557/12 consulta on letters.

[37] *Tudor and Stuart Proclamations* 1, no. 981; see also Tierney-Dodd, 4: p. lviii.

[38] *A Supplication* . . . pp. 3, 9, 10. See Allison and Rogers, p. 44 for identification of Colleton.

[39] *Journals of the House of Commons* 1: p. 144.

It was an appeal, not to theology, but to the practice of the law courts.

The House received this advice with poorly concealed resentment, but it had other matters of greater urgency to occupy its early weeks. There was the unpopular union with Scotland to be debated, the question of the subsidy to the Crown to be weighed, and a strenuous attempt to curtail the influence of the Anglican episcopacy to be made. Finally on April 16, Sir Francis Hastings moved the establishment of a select committee to consider "the confirmation and reestablishment of religion, maintenance of a learned ministry and whatever else may bring furtherance therunto." There was still no attempt to raise the question of the Catholics as such, except that on one occasion a delegation from the Commons which had met with delegates of Convocation later complained—rather strangly—that "Papists get too much encouragement out of Convocation House." [40] The Commons would finally reach the question of recusancy laws in mid-June during the peace conference with Spain.

Ever since the opening of Parliament Juan de Tassis had kept to his task of attempting to foster good relations, chiefly with the Privy Council, while trying to offer excuses for the absence of the Constable of Castile to King James. It was becoming increasingly difficult. On March 22, three days after James's speech to the Commons, Tassis advised the Constable that the King was insisting on the presence of his principal ministers in London during the present session of Parliament and there could not be a conference outside of England. He politely pleaded that the Constable should come as soon as possible but he hastened to add that he would make no announcement until he had explicit word from him. To prod the dallying Spanish envoy, James had publicly said that eight councilors were being considered as commissioners for the treaty. Two of these, Hume and Kinloss, were Scotsmen, and Tassis reported that he had found them the most amiable of the group. In this dispatch Tassis emphasized that James's friendship for Spain was virtually assured, but that he still was afraid of the opposition of Robert Cecil. He told the Constable that the secretary was "the sage of the English Court and very powerful." He explained: "When Aremberg arrived here he found him, as I did later, very reluctant to have peace and already under obligation to the [Dutch] rebels . . . I believe the credit that he has with the king comes more from necessity rather than affection." [41] For the present Tassis felt that his only hope was in the Countess of Suffolk who claimed to have great influence over Cecil, and so he hoped to "capture" her services with gifts. He had decided, rather foolishly, that the Countess was secretly a Catholic but he was sure that Cecil was "as heretical as Satan." He had concluded that there was nothing

that would move Cecil unless "his master"—the King —should force him, or the Countess could persuade him.

The month of April was probably the most difficult of all of Tassis' troubled embassy. He had not heard from the Spanish court for two months, and the Constable's policy of waiting left Tassis the responsibility for all the preliminary negotiations. He was bargaining secretly without adequate powers, and his work could always be vetoed by the Constable. Finally Philip III sent an answer to the January dispatches of Tassis; he commended the envoy for his work and advised him not to discourage the Catholics, or give them any cause to believe that Spain had abandoned them, as if they were a group of little strength or importance. On the contrary if he met any of their leaders he was to tell them that the Constable of Castile had been ordered "to procure their benefit." Furthermore he should remind them that, since Clement VIII had ordered them to obey King James, the Spanish ambassador would now be better able to "intercede on their behalf." [42]

Thus with only this vague generality to guide him Tassis approached the time for the actual conference to begin. On May 17 the Archduke's commissioners arrived. Richardot, Vereyken and Aremberg had left Gravelines the preceding week under the escort of an English squadron. Pleading ill-health the Constable of Castile had remained in Flanders after delegating his powers as a commissioner to Tassis and to a trusted Milanese lawyer in his suite, Senator Alessandro Robida. The substitute Spanish commissioner reached London in company with the Archduke's envoys.

As a token of honor to Spain, King James had lavishly furnished a large suite in Somerset House and for greater convenience had placed the meetings of the conference in a few rooms set aside in the same building. It was rare to hold peace negotiations in the palace of the visiting ambassador and it was an embarrassing affront to learn that the Constable had still not arrived. His deliberate waiting had some justification at this time, however, since it was calculated to seek a better bargaining position for Philip and the Archduke. The offensive of Ambrosio Spinola at Ostend and in the Ecluse was still not completed but it promised to be a notable Spanish victory. Moreover, Philip III had still to authorize all the money needed to fulfill the pensions planned by Tassis. In fact Philip still had to answer the Constable's request for final instructions. [43]

The initiative for holding the conference at this earlier date had probably come from the Archduke for his

40 *Ibid.*, pp. 172, 234–235.

41 E 841/17.

42 E 2571/69.

43 Folger MS. G.b.5 f. 39 v "Relación de lo que a passado en lo de la Paz. . . ." See Mattingly's description of the volume, in which this excerpt is found, in *Aspects de la propagande Religieuse* (Travaux d'Humanisme et Renaissance, **28**, 1957). p. 325.

envoys were given their final instructions by April 12. His commissioners were told to seek to curtail the English assistance to the Dutch both militarily and commercially, and especially to try to end the English occupation of the cautionary towns. As to the English Catholics the Archduke told them: "As the King our brother has ordered his own envoys to handle this, you are to leave this matter to them . . . aside from helping them quietly in it, in whatever way they propose." [44]

Since the Constable stayed in Flanders, Tassis assumed the role of principal commissioner and settled into the apartments prepared by King James in Somerset House. On May 19 James announced the authorization of five of his Privy Council—the same number as the foreign delegates—to be his commissioners for the conference. They were Thomas Sackville, Earl of Dorset, Charles Howard of Effingham, Earl of Nottingham, Charles Blount, Earl of Devonshire, Henry Howard, Earl of Northampton, and Robert Cecil, Viscount Cranbourne. [45]

IV. THE CONSTABLE OF CASTILE'S DECISION, MAY–AUGUST, 1604

The spring of 1604 was a time of false alarms and misleading rumors over the impending negotiations. Earlier in the year there had been printed in Lisbon a short narrative of the first months of the residence of Tassis in England. The little book dwelt largely on the first ceremonial audience granted by King James, with a gossipy attention to names, clothes, and jewels. The writer conveyed the impression that England was anxious to honor Spain and that a total success for its embassy was imminent. There was even a bogus news item: ". . . . in a dispatch of November it was learned that the king has ordered the release of all Catholics in prison, a thing which has sorely grieved the Puritans." In London other strange reports were current. Tassis wrote, in considerable pique, that it was being said that 500,000 escudos were at his command as an offering for peace. [1]

King James was not deceived by such rumors, yet he apparently had some second thoughts about his open appeal to the Commons to use "reason" on the Catholic question. He was reliably reported to have been alarmed that Catholics were increasing in numbers and the open practice of their religion; he wished laws "to hem them in." It looked as if the task of Tassis and Robida had become impossible.

The conference was to meet in eighteen sessions from May 20 to July 6; the intervals were used to allow the English commissioners to consult King James, and

both sides to prepare their positions. [2] The first two meetings were wasted on James's doubts over whether his honor would be satisfied with Tassis and Robida as substitutes for the absent Constable. He decided that it was. It was also agreed that the treaty was to deal with a "peace of fine amity and friendship with condition not to attempt anything to each other's prejudice or wrong." This was a compromise that obviously excluded the offensive and defensive alliance which would have had to stipulate the end of English intervention on behalf of the Dutch. The rest of the meetings turned consistently to commercial and military arrangements. Ten of the sessions touched various aspects of the Dutch rebellion, while the rest dealt with trade with Spain, the Low Countries and the Indies. The problem of the Inquisition was discussed in the fourteenth session and an article agreed upon. The diary makes it clear that for this session Tassis and Robida handled all the discussions for the one side, and Robert Cecil and Henry Howard for the other. The reasons for this grouping are not hard to find. Cecil, as his father before him, knew Spanish well. He owned Spanish documents which he gave to Hakluyt for his collection and he had followed Spanish affairs carefully through his agents. It was not an idle flattery that William Stepney dedicated one of the earliest Spanish grammars to him. Similarly, Henry Howard had translated Charles V's famous final instructions for Philip II. During this conference, when he argued for the rights of England to trade in the Indies, he cited two Spanish histories to aid his argument. [3]

By the middle of the conference a personal antipathy of Richardot for Tassis had begun to manifest itself quite openly. It appeared that the initiative in declaring the Hapsburg priorities in the north was regularly taken by the Spanish envoys to the annoyance of the delegates from Brussels. On June 23 Richardot complained to the Archduke that his interests were poorly protected in London: "as if everything came from the King, and nothing from your Highness." He added that the English commissioners were privately mocking his delegation by implying that the transfer of sovereignty of 1598 in the Low Countries had only been a pretense. [4] What Richardot did not explain on this occasion was that the English Commissioners were very mindful of the strong sympathy for the Dutch in the House of Commons. It can be doubted whether Richardot on his own could have obtained any concessions in the crucial matter of the Anglo-Dutch alliance. The Venetian Ambassador at this time reported to the Doge that a motion had been made in the Commons asking

[44] P.E.A. reg. 358 f. 400 v.

[45] *Rymer, Foedera* **16**: pp. 580–581.

[1] Anon., *La Segunda Parte de la Embaxada de Don Juan de Tassis, Conde de Villa Mediana.* . . . Sig 4v; E 841/17.

[2] "Diary of Proceedings," copy, Earl of Jersey MS. *H.M.C. 8th Report, Appendix I,* pp. 95–97; see also Gardiner, **1**: pp. 202–204.

[3] G. Ungerer, *Anglo-Spanish Relations in Tudor Literature,* pp. 53 ff. (Schweizer Anglistische Arbeiten) Band 38, Bern, 1956; *H.M.C. 8th Report,* p. 97.

[4] P.E.A. liv. 364 f. 132.

the Speaker humbly to approach King James to state their interest in preserving the rights and privileges of the Dutch.[5]

The silence in the formal sessions of the conference on the question of the Catholics was noticeable. Although Philip III had placed a high priority on it in his instructions to Tassis, a plausable explanation for the absence of discussion would be that the final action of Parliament was being awaited. After only four sessions of the conference, a bill requiring the execution of the Elizabethan statutes against Catholics had been introduced into the House of Lords on June 4. The outspoken—but solitary—opposition of Lord Montague had been muted by his temporary arrest and confinement in the Tower. By the end of that week the bill had been sent to the Commons, where a large committee made several emendations. After passing both houses it was given the royal assent on July 4. In its final form this act reaffirmed all of the Elizabethan statutes, and established new penalties for attending the English colleges on the continent.[6] To placate the foreign ambassadors James assured the French envoy —and through him indirectly Venice and Spain—that he had no intention of enforcing the statutes but he had the power should need arise.

Juan de Tassis kept the Constable informed of the significant developments in Parliament. Writing from Bruges at the end of June, when the attitude of both houses of Parliament had been made clear, the Constable told Philip III that there was not much left but hope for the better treatment of Catholics. He recalled the warning signals of the past months: the edict of March expelling priests, the recent anti-Catholic speeches in Parliament, and now the fresh confirmation of the recusancy laws. He agreed with Tassis that at present the Puritans were going to have their way. His only recourse appeared to be an approval of the Tassis' plan to distribute gifts, bribes and pensions lavishly at court. By this he hoped to reduce the threatened rigor against Catholics.[7]

For the time being the quiet work of Tassis had become the only feasible procedure, yet the blow was a bitter one to English Catholic hopes. Henry Garnet reported to Rome that all the penal laws were being confirmed and the hope for liberty of conscience was slight: "Dr. Taylor says that the reason is that the Spaniards do not give a farthing."[8] As a last effort, another petition had been presented to King James. Several weeks later it was printed at a secret press in London, with a false imprint at Douai, under the title: *A Petition Apologeticall presented to the Kinges most Excellent Majesty by the Lay Catholics.* Its purpose was to recall to King James the support of Catholics

in advancing his rights to the throne and to protest his patronage of anti-Catholic tracts. It noted "the new decrees and burdens" which were being planned in Parliament "for the reviving of the former capital lawes and pecuniary payments . . . rather charging us with a heavier hand than easing us of our former burdens. . . ." It asked that their rights of conscience should be protected.[8a]

However, Parliament was determined to have its way and King James would not press the issue. If anything at all was to be attempted, secrecy was vital. At this time Tassis explained his activities in a dispatch in cipher to Philip III. He implied that at present it was sufficient to make a concession to England in the secret protocol which restored the Alva-Cobham agreement of 1576 restraining the jurisdiction of the Spanish Inquisition.[9] For the present it was more important to prepare a complete list of suggested gifts and bribes for the approval of the Constable and the Spanish Council of State.

On June 28 Tassis dispatched to the Constable at Bruges the list of the names of the courtiers who should be rewarded: "in return for what had been done and what will be done." He was clearly implying in these words that some of them were involved in a private negotiation. He noted that the public sessions of the treaty would soon be finished and "those who have placed some stone in this edifice are anxious to know what prize or reward they have to draw out."[10] Tassis had become convinced that several English courtiers were sincere in saying that they were running a heavy risk in showing publicly any favor to Spain, but he was still shrewd enough in certain obvious cases, such as Henry Howard's, to question their full reliability. He ended his letter with a timely warning to the Constable to make sure of his letters of credit before arriving in England. His estimate of the English Court at the time of the treaty is a valuable record of the reactions of the Spanish ambassador to a year's experience of England; yet it can be best understood in its context with other contemporary dispatches.

The Spanish ambassador began with a suggestion that the Earls of Dorset, Devonshire, and Nottingham should be given pensions of 3,000 escudos a year, with Dorset to be honored with a special additional gift of 2,000 escudos as a further reward. Northampton, because "he has served me well," was to receive 5,000 escudos and in addition a "gift" which was not given a stated value. Robert Cecil was to be given a pension of 3,000 escudos which the Constable noted was to be raised to 6,000. Tassis' comment on Cecil's role in the negotiations was very revealing:

He has not done the harm that he was supposed to do. . . . It is better to leave him satisfied and to satisfy whomever

[5] *Cal. S.P. Venetian* **10**: pp. 157–158.

[6] *Journal of the House of Commons* **1**: pp. 247–248; *Statutes of the Realm*, 1 Jac. I, c. 4.

[7] E 841/71.

[8] *A.R.S.J.* Anglia 38–II f. 176.

[8a] J. Lecey, *A Petition Apolegeticall . . .* , pp. 8–10.

[9] E 841/80.

[10] E 841/117.

he desires. . . . I wish that he be given some secret compensation, for as he is to remain first secretary of State with his hand in everything, he will remain friendly and will not turn from us.[11]

For the Earl of Northumberland there should be a gift of 4,000 escudos, for the Earls of Cumberland and Suffolk a gift of 3,000 escudos. The Earl of Worcester was to be given merely some small gift in public; he was described as doing nothing to help a peace with Spain. The list continued with smaller gifts suggested for various Scottish lords and other royal officials. In many of the suggestions, it was obvious that the ambassador was simply following the custom of the times. Yet the effect of his largesse would be described later by the Venetian Ambassador: "The Spaniards are lauded to the skies, for in fact this is a country where only those who are lavish are held in account; and since my arrival in Court ten months ago, I have heard of nothing so often as presents." [12]

Most of the gifts so far described were fairly predictable. The two most interesting personal reactions of Tassis should now be examined. He had become convinced that, after Robert Cecil, Sir Thomas Lake was the most important official at court. He asked the Constable's advice as to his pension and remarked "he is said to be a Catholic, but not in public." Lake was to continue to be a friend of the Spanish ambassador for many years. Moreover, to the unconcealed irritation of the Constable, Tassis had kept a favorable view of the work of his confidant, the Countess of Suffolk. She had become the most important personage in terms of monetary reward: 20,000 escudos in cash, and in addition, three jewels worth 16,000 escudos were requested. Tassis' correspondence had not carefully indicated what especially the Countess had done that merited such an unprecedented expenditure. The Constable dismissed the idea of rewarding the Countess as serving her ambitious avarice. In a letter to King Philip III he observed: "Although I do not dismiss the advice of this confidant that offers liberty of conscience, she has so far given little foundation for it." He disliked her,

no less for her excessively grand pretentions . . . as well as for her capricious requests. . . . Recently she has demanded of the Count of Villa Mediana the purchase, on the chance of the success of the negotiations, certain jewels worth up to 16,000 scudos, she is pressing him that he give her one of them at once, which I believe would be worth 4,000.[13]

In replying to Tassis the Constable asked for further reasons for rewarding the Countess, as well as an explanation for the rest of his ambitious schedule of gifts and bribes. He still was not sure that such an outlay was being made at a justifiable risk. Tassis answered rather vaguely that the full details could not be given as yet, but he gave a general excuse:

Concerning the report of deserving people which I have sent to your Excellency I admit that it is large, for it contains something from justice, and much from gratuity. There had to be placed in it everything that comes from courtesy and presentation, and what passes here for bribe and pension. It is well understood that it must be for only the point of religion . . . even should it be for watching over things only in the future it can not be a small amount. The benefit that the Catholics will receive is unknown. I am waiting to see what the Lady will tell me, later I understand that she will speak with more clarity in this matter. I can not satisfy at present your Excellency's question nor send my opinion about what the money will procure.[14]

The plan apparently was leaked to other people first. An early hint can be seen in a letter of Henry Garnet of July 17 to the Papal Nuncio in Flanders, Ottavio Frangipani. He told him that the "principal councillors give their oath that, on the prompt payment of 200,000 escudos, all the monetary fines will be relaxed against Catholics . . . for twenty years." Garnet requested once again that strong diplomatic efforts be made in Rome and Madrid to secure this payment, which if necessary could be repaid later by the English Catholics. The Nuncio in Brussels was coldly indifferent to this promising news from England. He did not, apparently from his other letters, have much reliance on Spain's good intentions. When, after a considerable delay, he passed the news to Cardinal Aldobrandino he remarked that he had no faith in its usefulness. He had word that the Constable of Castile had the details of the same offer, and he implied that he did not expect a cooperative effort on the part of Rome and Spain.[15]

The notion of paying in advance for toleration, by satisfying the recusancy fines, was not as simple a solution as might at first appear. While the complex problem of the manner of enforcement of the anti-Catholic laws in the late Elizabethan and Jacobean periods needs much careful study, there are sufficient indications at present that the rigor in enforcing them, and especially in preparing the indictments and, on conviction, in exacting the recusancy fines depended on circumstances of the locality and people involved. Some local justices were reluctant to enforce them; there are many letters from the Privy Council urging them to do their duty. In certain localities they evidently were not. Even in the payment of fines, compositions for less than the amount of the penalty were permitted. As early as 1586 there were lists drawn up showing the names and sums offered and the substantial difference from the original fines. In one year when £11,924 were expected, £3,198 were actually collected.[16] In effect, these cases involve individuals whom the court for various reasons was not anxious to pursue too rigorously. Yet, there still remained the serious threat of economic ruin which was the basis of the coercive policy against Catholics.

---

[11] E 841/118 and 99.

[12] Cal. S.P. Venetian 10: p. 179.

[13] E 841/71.

[14] E 841/78.

[15] Frangipani Correspondence 3(2): pp. 725 ff. and 485 ff.

[16] Cal. S.P. Dom. 1581–1590, pp. 331, 365. See Dietz, English Public Finance, pp. 53–54.

In the last two decades of Elizabeth's reign there had been created through the recusancy laws a new source of revenue for a Crown which was increasingly hard pressed for cash. Moreover, the Draconian character of some of the laws had allowed the growth of a second source of revenue for private individuals. For on the one hand there were the bribes and private agreements made with Crown officials by which some recusants obviously escaped heavier penalties; and on the other there were the large investments that some favored individuals had made in the leasing from the Crown of the temporarily sequestered lands of recusants.[17]

Thus, financially, the recusancy laws meant additional revenue to the Crown and profits to certain favored individuals. Any secret plan, such as the one hinted at in the Tassis correspondence, had, at least, to offer a suitable sum to make the Crown abandon its former source of revenue. It was already well known that King James had remitted a large percentage of the fines so that for the first two years of his reign the income from the recusants was roughly a fifth of its usual amount. But there was no guarantee that this would continue, instead the signs of James's desire "to hem them in" were becoming more evident. Thus, the timing of the secret Spanish offer for the closing of Parliament's session and the ending of the treaty conference becomes more understandable. Under parliamentary pressure King James was presented with a full endorsement of the laws against Catholics. Moreover, the Commons had refused the impecunious King a sorely needed subsidy.

It was a very tempting offer: James might even enlarge his policy of excusing fines to the Catholic laity. Spain was offering 200,000 escudos—close to £48,000 —for twenty-one years of freedom from the enforcement of the laws. The sting of the Commons' refusal to grant a subsidy was being nicely soothed. Later in September, 1604, the Earl of Dorset, the Lord Treasurer, would point out to the King that there was revenue in anti-Catholicism: "Sire, it is necessary that there be an increase in either papists or puritans. I prefer the increase of Papists . . . for they are peaceful people, and in their increase your Majesty will derive much money."[18]

The Constable's letter, late in July, showed a reserved enthusiasm for Tassis' secret negotiation. On July 25 he remarked to Philip III that his information from England had convinced him that Parliament was strongly Puritan and reluctant to see peace with Spain.

He apparently had grasped the fact that King James could not annul the recusancy laws without parliamentary approval, and this was now out of the question. He had decided that the most that James could do would be to grant some favor to the Catholics in secret. He now told Tassis to arrange for this by discussions, gifts, and other means so that in the future, perhaps in another Parliament, "there might be done what was impossible in this." The Constable declared that he would go to England "when this plan has more force."[19]

Tassis and the Countess must have been working with considerable speed for the Constable was able to report from Dunkirk on July 30 that the "negotiations of all things that do not require my presence" had been ended in the preceding week. By then the offer of the Countess had become very explicit: "By payment of 192,000 escudos we can redeem the payments of twenty one years for the Catholics." This posed the problem of the additional letters of credit that were already authorized but had not been delivered. Fortunately, two days later the authorization for 200,000 escudos would be issued by the Centurioni brothers in Antwerp. The Constable had found the latest dispatches from Tassis encouraging, for he wrote that the Countess had promised that Catholics would be allowed to live in peace in their homes. It showed how much the two Spanish envoys had learned in eighth months that a concession, which they had once thought unworthy of the English Catholics, should now be so eagerly grasped. "One of the most important men at Court will come to see me and clear the matter up," he concluded, as he prepared for his coming journey to London.[20] He expressed the hope that the Papacy would assist in some discreet way, but it was almost as an afterthought, for he did not view Clement's help very enthusiastically.

On August 5 the Constable landed at Dover. His normal skepticism had returned to him in the interval as he prepared for traveling on to London. He wrote two brief notes to Philip at this time. In one he acknowledged the new letters of credit for 200,000 escudos "which your majesty has been pleased to send me for the English negotiations."[21] In another he remarked that there was no hope for changing the lot of the Catholics but that he would sign the treaty as he knew Philip would not wish negotiations to be broken off. Even if the Catholic leaders suggested a delay so that James would be forced to make some gesture, the Constable said he would refuse. He felt that such a delay would only add to the Catholics' "afflicted state." He wrote this with some regret, but "I see no powerful faction, no victorious army ready in Flanders, no fleet prepared. . . ." Then he complained again of the aloof attitude of Clement VIII.

[17] The excellent study of Prof. Joel Hurstfield has shown the economic reasons for the continuance of a similar abuse in the Court of Wards. See *The Queen's Wards*, pp. 329–347; M. J. Havran, "Sources for Recusant History among the Bankes Papers in the Bodleian," *Recusant History* 5(1960): pp. 246–255; H. Aveling, *Post Reformation Catholicism in East Yorkshire*, pp. 21–46.

[18] E 841/184. See appendix.

[19] E 2557/20.

[20] E 841/112.

[21] E 842/165.

I see that the Pope himself, whose principal concern should be this very matter, is not only silent but advising that the peace conference must not be broken off since nothing can be done in the matter of religion. It is not possible to be worse off than we are at present. The papacy is the true portal through which the affairs of the Catholics should be arranged.[22]

The reaction of the Council of State in Spain to the promising developments in England was equally skeptical. All of the principal terms of the treaty had been sent to them, as well as the secret plans of the Countess of Suffolk. However, their discussion was delayed in timing until the actual signing had taken place. The Council had already approved of the treaty, it was still concerned about the hope of toleration. Juan de Idiaquez was dubious of the usefulness of the Countess' plan to remit the fines for twenty-one years. He noted that Parliament had made it clear to King James that the recusancy laws were not to be relaxed. Since Philip was aiming at an effective and legal toleration, Idiaquez suggested that the Constable should be ordered to negotiate a settlement similar to the edict of Nantes. Thus he wished that the Catholics should be given assigned localities where they could exercise their religion publicly. To gain this, he observed, even double the present sum of £48,000 would be well spent.

The other Councilors commented on the plans of the Countess of Suffolk and Juan de Tassis with less enthusiasm. The Marquis of Velada said frankly he did not trust anyone at the English court, for even if the money were paid, the English would find a way to persecute the Catholics. The Count of Chinchon pointed out that everything seemed to hang "on the word of a fickle woman." If the money were to be paid, he warned, it must be paid directly to the Catholics; otherwise the Countess would keep too much for herself. The Count of Miranda was worried that Spain, after promising to help the Catholics some time ago, would now suffer the "loss of its good name." The Duke of Sessa seemed to feel the entire negotiation of the treaty was being handled too rapidly; he inquired why the Constable was in England if the King and his Council showed such disappointment over its provisions. He felt certain that nothing was going to be done for the Catholics, as the laws recently passed "in front of the very beards of your Majesty's envoys" proved that the Catholics' hopes in Spain had been wasted.[23] The only notation that King Philip wrote on this memorandum of disapproving opinion was that his Council was to await further word from London.

From the time of the Constable's arrival in England on August 5 until his departure on August 30 every public ceremony was carefully noted. Two full accounts were later published in Spanish, for the interest in this historic occasion was not confined to England. The color of his cordial and sumptuous reception in England should not distract from the obvious political significance of this visit. An important period of Anglo-Spanish friendship was beginning, and it would outlast the life span remaining to each of the Commissioners present at Somerset House in London.

The arrival of the Constable was really the foundation of one of the important political cliques within the English court during the reign of James I: the "Spanish faction." When the Constable set foot in England he brought letters for credit for approximately £100,000, and he intended to do two things. The first was the usual presentation of gifts publicly at Court while he privately approved the secret but regular pensions to a selected group of courtiers. He expected, correctly, to have little difficulty in this matter. His second objective was the far more difficult one of buying the remission of recusancy fines. His selected list of courtiers—even though it was only expected of them to favor Spanish interests against the diplomacy of the United Provinces or of France—would be of still greater importance in any such undertaking.

What was the quality of the pro-Spanish sentiment at James's court at the time of his arrival? Of the five commissioners of peace, three—the Earls of Dorset, Northampton, and Devonshire—had been described, after several months of observation by Tassis, as more inclined to Spain than to France. The Earl of Nottingham, despite his lucrative post as Lord High Admiral, had abandoned the war faction and was inclined to make peace with Spain. The Constable did not trust him at this time but later they were to become more cordial in Spain. Robert Cecil was neutral. It is evident that the Constable shared the opinion of the Venetian Ambassador who had decided that Cecil was favoring peace *faute de mieux,* he would have opposed it "had the Crown not been in straits for money on account of the late wars."[24] With this significant exception therefore the English commissioners were really inclined to peace, and three had given clear signs of being friendly to Spain's interests. Outside of the Somerset House delegates there were other influential courtiers. There were the Earl and Countess of Suffolk. The Earl, Tassis had noted to the Constable, would follow Cecil's lead; yet "he has always tried to satisfy me." Despite the Constable's unconcealed dislike for the Countess, she was a valuable confidant. Sir Thomas Lake was known to favor the peace but his pro-Spanish sentiments were as yet untested.

There were additional minor figures of interest on whom the Constable could safely rely for some support. There was the pro-Spanish sentiment of three ladies of the Court: Lady Drummond and the Countess of Bedford, the confidants of Queen Anne, and Penelope Rich, the mistress of the Earl of Devonshire; but he had no idea what influence they would ultimately have. There had also been very promising signs from four

22 E 842/162.
23 E 2557/21.

24 *Cal. S.P. Venetian* **10**: p. 176.

of James's Scottish favorites, who were definitely inclining toward Spain at that time; Lord Hume, the lay Abbot of Kinloss, Sir John Ramsey, and Sir James Lindsey.

As a "faction" the courtiers were not numerically strong. On examination, its leadership rested within the Howard circle principally, and this was not a family of inflexible loyalties to any causes except to its own interests. Howard of Effingham, Howard of Marn Hill, and Howard de Walden were not going to risk anything substantial for Spain, but their friendship was not to be neglected. In a country tired of the costs of a war, which in nineteen years had become an expensive stalemate, the Howards had entered the peace party. The King was known to favor peace, and it was a more popular cause to follow at the moment. When James had required for his service an oath which was against a Catholic's conscience, these three Howards had taken it, but they had made it clear to Tassis that they would prefer to end the recusancy laws only at the suitable time.

Early in his brief stay in England the Constable evidently decided that he should not pursue, at the present, the secret objective of buying toleration. He told Tassis, however, to continue the secret negotiations which, as shall be seen, were to be prolonged for almost a whole year. He turned to the business at hand: the ceremonies of ratification and the bestowing of gifts.

In London the Constable approved two secret protocols which had been prepared provisionally by Tassis and Robida. The first consisted of two articles granting English ships the right to bring German merchandise to Spain free of the usual 30 per cent impost. The second was the more famous one on the Inquisition

Fig. 1. The Commissioners for the Treaty of London, Somerset House, August, 1604. Attributed to Marcus Gheeraedts II. *Left to right*: Louis Vereyken, *Audiencier* of Brussels; Jean Richardot, President of the Privy Council; Charles de Ligne, Count of Aremberg; Alessandro Robida, Senator of Milan; Juan de Tassis, Count of Villa Mediana; Juan de Velasco, Duke of Frias, Constable of Castile; Thomas Sackville, Earl of Dorset; Charles Howard, Earl of Nottingham; Charles Blount, Earl of Devonshire; Henry Howard, Earl of Northampton; Robert Cecil, Viscount Cranbourne. By courtesy of the National Portrait Gallery, London.

renewing the Alva-Cobham 1576 agreement, except for one article which had previously insisted that English residents in Spain—in distinction to itinerant merchants —were subject to the same laws as Spanish subjects.[25] There was a definite false impression on the English side that the Constable was possibly violating Philip's instructions in granting the protocol. This was untrue, as the Council of State had voiced no objection prior to his arrival in England.[26]

When published in English one year after the treaty, this protocol stated that no English man would be subject to the Inquisition: "if they have exceeded in any thing before their entrance into Spaine." While there was no compulsion to enter churches, if they did so they were obliged to show suitable reverence. Similar deference was required in the presence of a procession of the Blessed Sacrament. Finally, if any Englishmen were found guilty of heresy, the authorities were "only to sequester their own proper goods" and not the whole ship and cargo which did not belong to them in any case.[27]

With the approval of the Treaty articles and the protocols, the visit of the Constable became perforce a largely ceremonial affair. The ratification was quickly arranged and King James, who had been away hunting during the first four days of the Constable's stay in London, returned to Whitehall to greet the long overdue Spanish ambassador. On Thursday, August 15, he received the Constable in a private interview which lasted an hour and a half.[28] There were many rumors in London as to what was discussed, and later the Constable reported that the return of the cautionary towns was mentioned, but that he would leave a fuller summary for his return visit to Spain.

On Sunday, August 16, the Earl of Devonshire led a suite of fifty gentlemen to escort the commissioners— except the ailing Aremberg—to Whitehall palace. There King James and his court led them to the Chapel Royal where Robert Cecil, after handing a copy of the treaty to the Constable, read aloud the oath by which the King and Prince Henry, their hands on the gospels, bound themselves to observe the peace with Spain.[29] The solemn ratifications at Brussels and Valladolid were to be held later.

The entire afternoon was taken up with an elaborate royal banquet to honor the Spanish embassy in the great hall of the palace. A table five yards in length was set up behind a railing to keep the curious crowd at a distance. At the head of the table under a cloth of state sat the King and Queen with the Constable on James's right, and the Count of Villa Mediana and Senator Alessandro Robida next to Anne. Prince Henry and the other commissioners occupied the remaining places. This was the occasion for calculated demonstrations of amity. An agate cup set with rubies in which the Constable first drank the health of their majesties of England, before presenting it to them, was valued at £3,000 in Antwerp. James was not to be outdone. He bestowed on the Constable a fine ring "for the marriage of peace" and a dinner service of gold and finally there was the "Royal Gold Cup," an unusually splendid example of medieval enamel work and the oldest item in the 1574 inventory of Queen Elizabeth's household treasure.[30] The Constable offered a present to Queen Anne in the form of a crystal cup carved as a dragon. After the banquet there was dancing, with the young Prince Henry being commanded by his parents to dance a "galliard" and a "correnta," and later the Earl of Southampton led Queen Anne in a "brando." Tiring of the dance, the brilliant assembly moved to the windows of Whitehall below which a vast crowd had assembled to watch the King's bears fight with the greyhounds.

Late that night the Spanish envoys were escorted back to Somerset House with a splendid company of fifty halbadiers lighting the route. As might be expected, King James was restless to leave London once more for hunting and later a royal progress to the north. Impatient to take the road at once, James visited the Constable at Somerset House the following day and then galloped off towards Rockingham with his hunting party. It was now the charge of Juan de Tassis to dispense the carefully planned public largesse of Spain for this great occasion.

The Countess of Suffolk received a gift of money close to £4,500 and jewels worth nearly £4,000 more. For Lord Robert Cecil and the Earls of Devonshire and Northampton there were jewels and gifts worth over £5,000. The Countess of Bedford and Lady Drummond each received gifts worth about £500. The final total of all gifts in the Constable's personal reckoning reached £36,000.

Yet there was a large unspent balance in these private accounts. It is evident that he refused to leave the letters of exchange for £48,000 to cover the recusancy fines since the discussions were judged to be still inconclusive. These letters were brought back to the Low Countries for the Council of State had been explicit that there had to be proofs of the mitigation of the treatment of Catholics.

Leaving London a few days later Tassis and the Constable traveled to Dover which they reached on August 30. On the way they prepared the list of pensions for influential courtiers which was to be sent to the Council

[25] E 2557/34: For the earlier agreement see *Cal. S.P. Spanish 1570–1579*, pp. 537–538, *Winwood Memorials* **2**: p. 29.

[26] *Winwood Memorials* **2**: p. 73; E 2557/21.

[27] "Three articles concerning a moderation to be had in the proceedings of the Inquisition . . ." in *Artices of Peace, Entercourse and Commerce . . .*, London, 1605.

[28] *Cal. S.P. Venetian* **10**: p. 178.

[29] *Cal. S.P. Venetian* **10**: pp. 178–179; *Frangipani Correspondence* **3**, 2: pp. 864–866.

[30] See *Notes and Queries* **222**: p. 170; A. J. Collins, *Jewels and Plate of Queen Elizabeth I*, pp. 279–281.

for final approval.[31] The list was small and the first instalment was due on January, 1605. The Constable apparently followed Tassis' opinion in nearly every case, for the names included Dorset, Nottingham, Devonshire, Northampton, Cecil, Suffolk, and his Countess of course, Hume, Kinloss, Lindsey, Lake, and Ramsey.

The departure of the Constable from London did not signify by any means, the ending of the secret efforts of Spain to acquire toleration, but for contemporary Catholic and Puritan alike his brief visit was the occasion for misunderstandings. Father John Gerard, a Jesuit working near London at that time, recalled later that many believed "that the Constable had received promises of toleration that were never kept." Much later John Lingard was to record in his *History* a tradition from contemporary narratives at his disposal that the Constable had made a personal appeal to James on orders from Philip III.[32] Francis Osborne—anti-monarchist and anti-Scottish—clearly recorded a Puritan belief in his *Traditionall Memorialls* that the Spanish were so anxious to have peace in 1604 "that they spared no cost to procure it." Moreover, Osborne believed that Philip III would not dare to ask for toleration, even if James had promised it before his accession.[33] Both Catholic and Puritan were wrong as to what the Constable and Don Juan de Tassis really were attempting to do. Neither King James nor any of his Council had made any official promises at this time in England. Toleration was put aside during the visit of the Constable because it had proved to be too ambitious a goal. The secret agreement about recusancy fines needed further precision and adequate guarantees. The Constable later confided to the Duke of Feria that even the Catholic leaders had agreed that a public stand at that time was impractical.[34] However, the misleading stories and rumors continued to provoke unrest.

The Constable was to remain several weeks in the Low Countries before returning to the Spanish court to report. In a letter written shortly after his arrival in Gravelines on September 12, he passed over the Catholic question with a promise that it would be explained in "a report which will be made when I see your Majesty." He gave, instead, many details of his quarrel with the Archduke over a debt of 40,000 escudos owed from the first letter of credit granted in November, 1603, at the start of his embassy.[35] Always

short of funds, the Archduke had refused to pay. Obviously he had decided that a large unspent surplus which the Constable had originally designated to pay the recusancy fines, could be well spent in the Low Countries.

In London money was also a problem. It was surely a striking coincidence that on August 22, 1604, after the refusal of the Spaniard to allow the payment of his promissary notes was known, the Privy Council was compelled to open negotiations for a loan of £20,000 with the Common Council of London.[36] It can be reasonably doubted that this would have been necessary had the Constable and King James reached an agreement. From one point of view, the Crown was for the first time paying a price for abiding by Parliament's will in the Catholic question.

V. THE PLAN COLLAPSES, SEPTEMBER, 1604–JUNE, 1605

After the Constable had embarked at Dover, Tassis returned to the English court to observe any signs of a new atmosphere. If he had any comment over the refusal of the Constable to become a *deus ex machina* for the tribulations of the English Catholics, he was careful to keep it out of his dispatches. He must have sensed, however, that the prospects for toleration were not bright. In London he discovered that the recently pledged amity was being confined largely to matters of commerce. It was the same in Spain. There the Council of State advised the Inquistor General that he should order his officials to use the greatest dispatch in visiting English shipping, and that proceedings should not be begun "from suspicions of small moment."[1] Robert Cecil confided to Sir Ralph Winwood, the English Ambassador to the United Provinces, that "sufficient satisfaction is obtained" by the secret protocol giving English merchants "further security." He was soon to report to Sir Thomas Parry in Paris that the merchants of London had been informed of all provisions of the treaty "so much as concerneth their trade and traffiq."[2]

The reopening of English trade with Spain was an opportunity for many sailors and itinerant merchants to satisfy an interest in Catholicism. In part these mariners merely reflected the increased activity among Catholics which was noticeable in England in the first years of James' reign. One English priest laboring in southern Spain reported to Father Joseph Creswell, who lived at the Spanish Court, that there were not enough priests who could speak English to meet the demand. Another, a Jesuit named William Johnson working in Malaga, complained to Creswell in November of 1604 that the local tribunal of the Inquisition

[31] E 2514/3 with memorandum of 9 September; the list has been summarized—inaccurately in places—in Gardiner, *History* 1: pp. 214–216, his transcripts made at Simancas are in B.M. Add. MS. 31,111.

[32] J. Morris, *Condition of Catholics under James I*, p. 72; J. Lingard, *History of England* (1883 ed.) 7: p. 46.

[33] *The Secret History of the Court of James the First* (1811 ed.) 1: pp. 153, 169–170.

[34] W.C.A., Series E vol. ii f. 202. Feria to Fitzherbert, letter of 2 November, 1604: "El Condestable añade que fue consejo de los mismos Catolicos no apretar por agora al Rey en materia de religion, por no ser ocasión para esto...."

[35] E 2584/98; see also *Notes and Queries* 212: 171.

[36] R. Ashton, *The Crown and the Money Market, 1603–1640*, pp. 114 ff.

[1] E 2512/13 consulta of 23 October, 1604.

[2] *Winwood, Memorials* 2: p. 28; S.P. 94/10/95.

was hindering his work by prolonging the process of reconciliation. He asked that an appeal be made to the Council of State against this policy and asserted that he had met many English sailors who wished to be Catholics; yet he felt that they should not be considered "heretics." Johnson explained that many of these Englishmen were so terrified of the Inquisition that he could do nothing with them. One of them, he wrote, had announced that "he would sooner walk barefoot to Rome"; a further complication was that many cases had to be settled in Granada which was a time-consuming distance from the coast and any one who went there would lose his place on the ship.[3]

The Council of State eventually considered this problem on December 16. Juan de Idiaquez voted to refer the complaint to the Inquisitor General with the advice to appoint special commissioners to handle the English cases without making it necessary to enforce the full requirements of the law. There was, however, no urgency in the wording the Council chose, and Philip III merely endorsed the *consulta* with a noncommittal note to advise the Inquisitor of the matter.[4] There it rested.

The situation in England was far less promising. Only two weeks after the Constable's departure King James issued a commission to Sir Thomas Egerton, then Lord Ellesmere, to preside over a large committee of privy councilors "to exterminate Jesuits." His motive was possibly to bolster the recent decrees of Parliament, but the wording of the commission does not give any special clue. There were the time-worn phrases about "Jesuits, seminary priests and divers other corrupt persons employed under colour of religion to withdrawe the hearts of our loving subjects from their allegiance toward us."[5] The commission included some councilors soon to be given Spanish pensions and who were clearly of moderate feelings in the matter. One of them, the Earl of Northampton, confided to Tassis that he had received a letter from Robert Cecil reporting many complaints that had been made directly to King James. These insisted that "the Count of Villa Mediana had given money to the Jesuits for the redemption of the Catholic payments." He told Tassis that he and his nephew, Suffolk, had to spend considerable time assuring the King that the story of money payments was a rumor spread by the French ambassador to destroy the success of the peace with Spain.[6]

Without a doubt the Catholic question was being discussed at the English Court and the need for some clearer policy was increasingly evident. King James summoned to Hampton Court on September 14 several members of the Privy Council to discuss a complaint by Catholics over the illegal imprisonment of recusants after they had paid their fines. It is quite probable that the source of this information to Tassis was again Henry Howard, the Earl of Northampton. He was to be a pensioner of Spain and in the only extant report of this meeting in Spanish he is made to appear in a favorable light.

The meeting began with a query from James for the opinion of the councilors about the Catholic complaint.[7] The discussion was opened by Northampton begging the King to follow his merciful inclination "and not to wash your hands in the blood of Catholics." Even Sir John Popham, the Chief Justice, advised that the justices could safely be moderate in treating Catholics who were not dangerous. Both Northampton and Cecil protested against this with the latter stating that he could not see the reason for rigor against Catholics "seeing that they govern themselves well and moderately and intend nothing against the state of our country." At this Cecil's older brother, Lord Burghley, disagreed, saying that Catholics would "incline more to the Pope . . . than to their Prince."

Northampton again spoke in favor of moderation saying that the cause of the Catholics was different from what it was in the time of Elizabeth "for many doubted her right to the throne because of her illegitimacy, further, she was excommunicated by the Pope and . . . at war with the king of Spain," whereas the present King of England was not in the same position. At this point James interrupted to say that Burghley had been well answered and he went on to remind the Council that his right to the throne was by other rights than Elizabeth's. To the opinion of Kinloss that an increase in the number of Catholics would be dangerous for they might wish to expel King James, Cecil replied:

I have no fear of the rebellion of Catholics for the sake of religion as I have never thought that any people has rebelled for the sake of religion, but more for policy and matters of state under pretext of religion. As the Catholics in the time of the late Queen have not rebelled, enduring such wretched oppression, it can be believed that being governed at present with love and gentleness they will not rise up nor rebel.

The discussion then turned to another aspect of the problem with the shrewd observation of Buckhurst that an increase of Catholics would mean more money in revenue to the Crown, while they continued their opposition to the Puritans. Suffolk, Northumberland, and Lennox also advised moderation in the Catholic question. The report concluded with the remark of King James that further debate would be needed, but for his part he would not have the priesthood made treason. The purpose of the King in holding the meeting was not

---

[3] E 842/10. Johnson entered the English college in Valladolid from the diocese of Chester in 1591; he gave an address of welcome to Philip II in 1592 in the Scots tongue. He became a Jesuit in 1596 and labored entirely in Spain where he died in 1614. (C.R.S. **30**: pp. 12–13.)

[4] E 2512/14.

[5] Rymer, *Foedera* **16**: pp. 597–599.

[6] E 842/21 consulta.

[7] E 841/184. See appendix for text.

made clear and, in any case, he was not to alter the lot of the Catholic laity because of it.

This report, as related to Tassis, is important primarily because it offers a rare opportunity to see what the Spanish ambassador, after his large expenditures, was told was the attitude of the Council on toleration. It would appear on this occasion to be a council that spoke only as James wished to hear it speak. The hope of toleration, or better, of leniency, was not entirely lost, but the Spanish Council of State, if it reflected on the contents of the Tassis message, must have seen that buying toleration was no longer a straight-forward affair of bargaining.

Finally an overture was made to Tassis with what evidently appeared to be James's knowledge. Early in October he reported that a new offer had been made to him concerning four limited points of toleration. It is not clear whether they were intended as a sop for all of Tassis' labors of the late spring climaxed by the largesse of the August ratification, or as a first step to later negotiations, or as a fraud to extort more Spanish gold. In any case, Tassis was told that the following four concessions were possible. First, that "there be no proceedings against the clergy and laity." A disappointingly vague promise which could hardly mean a repeal of the recusancy laws but in the light of the report from Hampton Court could mean that James intended to moderate the activities of the Justices. The second was that "the goods of Catholic recusants were not to be seized." This was in effect a vague promise that might have ended the abuses in the sequestration of the property of convicted recusants. The third was that "no one entering the ports [of England] be required to take the oath [of supremacy] except in suspicious cases." The fourth was that "catholic recusants cease being confined to their estates." This would imply the repeal of the notorious "five mile ordinance" of 1593. The four points thus came to two vague promises and two more specific pledges which were in themselves worthwhile, but unfortunately there were no clarifying details about enforcement, so that they remain quite difficult to evaluate accurately. Tassis merely stated that the "price" for these concessions was £2,000. He wrote: "the English do not press me for the money which I should offer at this time, but should they do so, I will be forced to give them something." He added that the discussions for the fines of twenty-one years were continuing.[8]

On learning of the plan the Constable was very hesitant to give his permssion to Tassis to agree to the bargain. He ordered Tassis on October 23 to get everything assured by a proclamation. His skeptical advice was to prove true:

I see no assurance for our expense but their word; and although that of a King and such important people could be trusted in very great matters, in the spending of money

8 E 843/79 consulta.

more resoluteness is necessary for the accidents that can happen.[9]

The insistence on the proclamation probably hastened the death of this curious plan for there is nothing more on these four points in the dispatches of Tassis. It would have been a token, and probably unofficial, alleviation of the anti-Catholic penalties while the heavy fines remained in force. The Spanish envoy turned to the negotiations for the twenty-one years of fines which were also discussed in two of Father Henry Garnet's letters of this time. Here there was a note of optimism which implied that the Catholics knew about them and were strangely confident of their outcome.

In his first letter Garnet urged the General of the Jesuits, Claudio Aquaviva, to ask the Pope to instruct the English Catholics to be patient in awaiting relief from the recusancy laws. Garnet seemed under the impression that the letters of credit the Constable carried to the conference were still in England, whereas they were actually with him in the Low Countries.

It would be convenient, [he reflected,] that in addition to the main amount of 50,000 pounds promised and left on deposit by the Constable towards toleration—this matter must be kept secret so that it be not taken ill that the Spaniards are known to be contributing the money—the Archpriest be given authority to impose on the consciences of the Catholics of England the payment of six to seven thousand pounds on account of the toleration. For otherwise, in my opinion, nothing will be done.

It was a large sum of money for the Catholics to try to gather. However, a week later, Garnet wrote that "the majority of Catholics praise highly the generosity of the king of Spain in having left, on deposit, the 50,000 pounds." The extant collection of Henry Garnet's letters is incomplete and his style is frequently so guarded that his meaning is not always clear, but while he did not refer to the matter again it is doubtful that Garnet was urging a supplementary payment. Undoubtedly, as he hinted, it was an ambitious project to repay some of the Constable's money, so that no link with Spain could be used to detract against it.[10]

The interest of Henry Garnet in this problem can be well appreciated when it is recalled that James, partly from his need of revenue and partly to satisfy the complaints of the Puritans, allowed the recusancy fines to be resumed in full rigor on November 28, 1604. These penalties were to yield over £2,200 by Easter of the next year.[11]

Meanwhile in Spain the attitude of the Constable towards the policy of Pope Clement was shared by the usually mild-mannered Philip III. The King was particularly irritated to learn that, although the Papacy had

9 E 841/191.
10 A.R.S.J. Anglia 38–II f. 176 v and 177–177 v, letters of 14 and 21 November, 1604.
11 Gardiner, History 1: p. 224; see Dietz, English Public Finance, p. 97, note 4, and Smith College Studies in History (1928) 13, no. 4.

not supported the Spanish plan to buy toleration, it should now inform the Spanish Ambassador, the Duke of Escalona, of its surprise that the Catholic King had done nothing to help the persecuted Catholics. The King drafted a note to the Duke that the Pope's nephew, Cardinal Aldobrandino, was to be informed of the true story and "should they charge you there with not having done more in the matter of religion you should speak of the offer of 200,000 escudos . . . there is a great difference in not attempting something and not succeeding in it." [12]

The disappointment of Philip III was evident to Tassis, for he made a point of reminding the King in his letter of December 23 that the Spanish Crown had tried as much as possible to procure a better situation for the recusants. He charged that the failure was because of the Puritans and "some Protestants who are the majority of the Council." They had informed the King apparently that the Spanish concern for the Catholics "was pointed to affairs of State and not of charity." He observed that great discretion was still vital: "I have proceeded so cautiously that even some of my Catholic friends at the outset thought ill of me for not looking into this negotiation." He felt—and with some justice—that all the English Catholics were too talkative, he wrote with some weariness: "even the Catholics and the Jesuits are a little imprudent in not knowing how to keep silent." [13]

Whatever their good intentions, some English Catholics clearly impeded the Spanish envoy who had to negotiate in secret. It was very likely that the plan of paying the fines in advance approved by the Constable in August, received more damage from the anti-Catholic sentiment reported by Northampton in September than Tassis had at first thought. Later there were to be the inquiries among recusants concerning the repayment of the Spanish money, which would also hurt the secrecy needed, if the plan were to mature.

The difficulties of their envoy were not well appreciated in Spain by the Council of State. In their meeting late in December, 1604, the members made impatient comments that Tassis' efforts to assist the Catholics were always ending in failure. They saw no need for secrecy in this matter "about which he ought to treat publicly with the king." [14] In the meanwhile, Tassis decided to keep to his policy of gaining the good will of the leaders of the Privy Council. The Spanish ambassador had been anxious to begin the pensions at once, but the Constable had warned that Philip's approval was still necessary for all the recommendations. [15] On the ninth of November Tassis advised King Philip that the pensions, planned to begin soon for five leading councilors, should be increased by the sum of 4,000

escudos. In his reply of February 3, 1605, the King agreed to the new sums but he warned once again not to dispense any largesse through the Countess of Suffolk "who would only keep half of it as she is so ambitious." [16] The ambassador was to repeat the same warning to Pedro de Zúñiga when he would arrive to take Tassis' place in July, 1605.

As in the preceding year, the months of December and January, 1604–1605, were a time of little activity. The only exception was that Tassis noticed an increased communication among the English Catholics; they were continuing to discuss the chances of paying the recusancy fines of twenty-one years. "They are now coming to me," he wrote, "to tell me that they are reckoning up to learn the total treasure they can produce alone to assure me of that amount." [17] They were particularly anxious to obtain a promise that, if the plan were approved by King James, it would apply not only to those who were contributing at present, but also to those who would show themselves as Catholics later. This latter group was understandably afraid that they would endanger their property by a future declaration.

It was not appreciated by Tassis that this inquiry over the status of future recusants was as crucial as it seemed. He made no comment upon it, and apparently considered it merely a slight additional favor to be granted by the King. In reality it was one of the most compelling reasons why the negotiations were always in doubt. It left James uncertain how to control the unknown strength of the Catholics once they could be revealed without any future reprisal.

By the middle of February, King James was faced with a dilemma. His main preoccupation had clearly become the Puritans, but it was evident that he could hardly be firm with them and still allow the Catholic recusants to go without prosecution. The King's problem was perfectly illustrated in the complaints of Archbishop Hutton. Within his sprawling province of York, Hutton had not been a vigilant prosecutor of those who would not accept the established church; in fact his lack of zeal and energy had prompted his removal as Lord President of the Council of the North. On that occasion Queen Elizabeth had remarked pointedly that her new appointee should now see to it that "by more vigilance and severity our people may be reduced from their defection." [18] But in the fall of 1604 when Hutton received orders from the Council to proceed against the Puritans and to see that men of adequate learning were presented to the various parishes, he wrote to Robert Cecil an impressive appeal for a more vigilant policy against Catholics. He first described the Puritans with an evident understanding:

The Puritans (whose fanatical zeal I mislike) though they differ in ceremonies and accidents, yet they agree with us in

[12] E 1857/403.
[13] E 841/197.
[14] E 842/21.
[15] E 841/190.

[16] E 2571/118.
[17] E 843/1.
[18] H. M. C. Salisbury MS. 9: p. 317.

substance of religion and I think all, or the most part of them, love his Majestie and the present state and I hope will yielde to conformitie.

However, he was far more disturbed about the Catholics whom he described as "opposite and contrary to manie very mayne points of religion." He observed that they "cannot but wish the Popes authorities and Popishe religion to be established," and he reminded Cecil that it was "high tyme to looke unto them, for verie many are gone from all partes to London, and some are come down into the countrie in great Jollitie and almost tryomphantly." He noted with distaste a rumor that Catholics were saying that the ecclesiastical commissions would not be renewed, and then gave an undeserved reproof to Robert Cecil: "If the Gospell quaile and Poperie prevaile, it will be primarily imputed to you, great Counsellor, who either excuse or yield to grant tolleracion to some." [19]

Robert Cecil already knew, even if Hutton could not as yet, that King James was even then being forced to agree to Hutton's sentiments, for very different reasons of state. However, Cecil freely expressed his own severe attitude in a reassuring reply to the Archbishop: "I love not to yield to all toleration. . . . I will be much less than I am, or rather nothing at all, before I shall ever become an instrument of such a miserable change." [20]

That letter was quickly followed by an official reminder from the King to Archbishop Hutton and Lord Sheffield informing them that "the scandalous rumours of my toleration are to be suppressed." [21] The more severe policy was soon made evident to the rest of England. By the clear encouragement of the Crown in the Spring of 1605 over 5,500 recusants were convicted. How many managed to escape by the usual underhand means cannot, of course, be estimated. But the surprising thing was that, according to Tassis, the Catholic leaders still continued to take the estimate of their resources as to how much they could offer in payment for the fines of twenty-one years. Their private inquiry was apparently finished by the middle of March. On the 17 of that month the Spanish envoy wrote to Philip that, after consultation they believed that £30,000 could be given, "if it should come to that point." [22] In the same letter he implied that, in order to succeed, he would have to work alone and avoid any further leaks and ruin the scheme by premature discovery. Clearly King James would not be able to complain of Spanish interference with his subjects if Tassis had his way. Yet because of his previous experiences, he was not overly optimistic; he only wrote guardedly of seeing whether "the door is still closed" on the point. He

asked King Philip to have consultations with the Council of State to learn how much he would be willing to offer. He observed, as if Philip needed a reminder, that nothing was done at the English Court except by money.

There was silence on the subject in Tassis' dispatches for nearly a month. In the meanwhile, Philip III had instructed him to seek the advice of Father Henry Garnet in this matter of the recusancy fines. Tassis had begun to probe the source of the claim of the Catholics to be able to pay £30,000. He had learned, he wrote to Philip, that the claim was based on the word of two Catholic gentlemen "of good reputation" who wished to remain anonymous. They had also made the surprising condition that Father Garnet was to have nothing to do with this negotiation. Their reason, as revealed to Tassis, was as petty as their offer was incredible. They said they did not wish the priest "to share in the merit of a work which they are doing before the Lord, nor that he should have the glory of being the one who terminated such a grand task." Tassis informed Garnet only of part of the offer as told to him. The Jesuit replied that he could not believe that any two of the Catholic gentry known to him could offer such a sum of money. He recalled that, as soon as it was rumored that the Constable had brought to England promissory notes for 200,000 escudos, several Catholics "began to withdraw from what they were thinking of giving."

To test the credentials of the two Catholic gentlemen, Garnet said he would place the names of six prominent Catholic gentry on a piece of paper. Should the two anonymous Catholics not be among them then Garnet advised that no credence be given to the offer. "I certify to your Majesty," Tassis wrote, "these two gentlemen were named among the six." He concluded his report with the remark that he had decided to continue the negotiation alone with these two gentlemen. [23] The Spanish envoy thought it would be easier in any event because he was always having difficulty in getting in touch with Garnet who could only be reached by a third party, "for he is always in hiding, or in flight."

Unfortunately this elusive, if exciting, incident is not mentioned again in Tassis' correspondence. Possibly it was as bogus as Garnet suspected. Certainly his disbelief in the offer of the enormous sum of £30,000 will be shared by many; and the petty reason for excluding Garnet hardly invites confidence. But the affair had another significance, Tassis would not be grasping at such doubtful expedients if the Countess of Suffolk were advising him. Evidently, for the time being, she was not offering encouragement, and Tassis was turning to even more unreliable confederates in order to act on the never abandoned instruction from King Philip that something should be done. However, the timing of the offer is still worth noting. The embassy of the Earl of Nottingham to Spain to secure

[19] Folger Library MS. V.a. 321 f. 38 v–39; E. Lodge, *Illustrations of British History* **3**: pp. 115–116; *Winwood, Memorials* **2**: p. 40.

[20] E. Lodge, *Illustrations of British History* **3**: pp. 128–129.

[21] *Cal. S.P. Dom. 1603–10*, p. 197.

[22] E 2584/4.

[23] E 2589/19.

the official ratification of the treaty of London had just begun. He had bade farewell to King James at Greenwich on March 21. There was the possibility that the Spanish Court would negotiate again for relief from the recusancy laws.

Apart from this slender chance, the late spring of 1605 was a period when Juan de Tassis was at his wit's end in following Philip's orders. Meanwhile, the Archduke Albert had appointed Conrad Schetz de Grobbendonck, Baron Hoboken, as his first ambassador to King James in March, 1605. Hoboken had been explicitly reminded to use "great circumspection in dealing with the Catholics, to listen to their complaints and be careful to counsel them to be patient, . . . to take care about those who say they are catholics, as they could also be spies." [24] The new Flemish ambassador, a protégé of Richardot, would hardly be anxious to assist Tassis because of the cool relationship that had developed between Brussels and Spain at the conference.

Similarly, the Papacy continued to follow an independent approach to England. Early in 1605 the mission of Sir James Lindsey to Rome had prompted another series of rumors about James's possible conversion, a new twist was added to the story since it was linked to the failure of the Constable in the preceding summer. The new version was that the Constable had been given private assurances of James's intentions and, therefore, had not pursued the Catholic question with full vigor. This was nonsense and certainly not confirmed by any of the extant dispatches of either Tassis or the Constable. The angry reaction of the Puritans to the creation in Rome of a committee of Cardinals to deal with English affairs, which was decided shortly after Lindsey's visit, did not promise any shift in the official policy towards Catholics. The aging and sickly Clement VIII still hoped that James would follow the same path as Henry IV of France twelve years before. Any close papal cooperation with Spain would be viewed with suspicion by France. It was to be only after Tassis had left England for good that under a new Pope, Paul V, word was sent to the Papal Nuncio in Brussels that no obstacle should be put in the path of Philip III to buy toleration. It was a grudging acquiesence and clearly implied that no cooperation had been offered prior to that time.[25]

The efforts of Tassis had come to nothing. However, it was not noticed at that time by the Spanish Council of State as the attention of both England and Spain became fixed on the embassy of Charles Howard, Earl of Nottingham, in the late spring of 1605. This was not a mere ceremonial visit but a carefully observed counterpart of the ratification at the Whitehall Chapel in the preceding summer. There was also to be a similar ceremony in Brussels where the Earl of Hertford witnessed the oaths sworn by the Archduke Albert and the Archduchess Isabella Clara Eugenia. The splendor of the Constable's public appearances in England had been memorable in London and James was anxious that England should create a similar impression in Spain. He also determined that the peace treaty should be ratified as soon as possible.

At least two contemporary narratives of the embassy were published to satisfy the curiosity of the English. *The Royal Entertainment of the Right Honorable the Earle of Nottingham sent Ambassador from his Majestie to the King of Spaine* was a short laconic diary containing merely a few lines about each day's events. The reader will agree with its unknown author who said quite honestly in the preface: "I am a better souldier than a scholler, therefore expect no eloquence." However, Robert Treswell's *Relation of such things as were observed to happen in the Journey of the right honourable Charles Earle of Nottingham* was a longer work offering many colorful details. It was written, according to the preface, to refute "the many false and ill contrived reports" about Howard's mission. It noted quite frankly James' command to imitate "how honourably and richly the Duke of Fryas . . . had formerly demeaned himself." Howard had followed these instructions with a lavish hand and assembled at Greenwich, on the twenty-first of March, a company totaling six hundred and fifty including:

Six trumpeters clad in orange colour damaske, with cloakes of cloth of the same colour and banners of damaske with his Honours armes thereupon. Six footmen in orange tawney velvet . . . six pages clad likewise in velvet of the same colour . . . thirty gentlemen with cloakes of black velvet, four score yeomen well appareled with livery cloakes of orange tawney cloth garded with silver and blue lace. . . .[26]

The splendid cavalcade needed seven ships to transport their belongings to Spain. There was also a strong retinue of noblemen. There were Nottingham's two sons and two nephews, Lord Willoughby and Lord Norris with his young gossiping secretary, Dudley Carleton, Sir Charles Cornwallis, who was to remain as resident ambassador at the Spanish Court, was there with his son, William, the future essayist. There were a number of other English gentry, many of them soldiers and mariners who had fought Spain in the Low Countries, or in the Portugal and Cadiz expeditions.

The Spanish expected the English to land at Santander but on the excuse that there were no pilots on board familiar with the Biscayan coastline Howard ordered the squadron to land at Corunna. He thereby added a tedious and expensive journey to their itinerary over the most difficult terrain on the peninsula. However, their reception was gratifying. The only discordant note in the happy company was struck by Sir Charles Cornwallis who was unwell and sulking over

---

[24] P.E.A. liv. 358 ff. 420–420 v.

[25] See *The Month* **63** (1888) : p. 61; S. Gardiner, *History* **1** : 224 ff.; *Recusant History* **5** (1960) : 201–202.

[26] *A Relation . . .* , pp. 1–5.

imagined affronts to his precedence within Howard's entourage.

Even before Howard had set out from England the Council of State in Valladolid had thoroughly debated the special problems that his embassy would present. Philip III was already determined to ratify the treaty articles and also to impress the embassy with Spanish hospitality. Even the question of the care of any English who might fall ill was examined and orders given to requisition a house in Valladolid if all the regular hospices were filled.[27] The consistent hints at a marriage alliance between Prince Henry and the Infanta were noted but it was decided that the question would not be discussed at all on this occasion. The mood of the Council was basically that the articles of the treaty were to be approved but interpreted strictly in matters of religion. There was considerable uncertainty as to what Howard would demand in matters of worship.

On March 12 the Constable, the Duke of Sessa and Juan de Idiaquez reviewed the thorny question of the privileges of an ambassador which they realized would have important consequences for the peace treaty. They could, perhaps, recall the rather dramatic incident of the expulsion of Doctor Man by Philip II during the period of peace with Queen Elizabeth. Idiaquez raised the difficulty that legally James, in virtue of his assumed powers over religion in England, could grant permission to the Spanish envoy to have the Mass privately in his residence in England, but Philip could not grant a similar freedom in Spain since such a permission rested only with the Papacy. The Constable and Sessa denied the interpretation of Idiaquez. They noted that there were still many enemies of the peace treaty who would be pleased that Spain had restricted the privileges of the English ambassador. They would be able to force James to denounce the treaty. Moreover, there was a matter of reciprocity, if the Spanish envoy had freedom in England—as did the envoys of Venice, France, Lorraine, and elsewhere—Spain should grant the same. It was decided that the secret treaty protocol concerning the rights of English merchants should be extended to the retinue of Howard. As a precaution a special message was sent to Juan de Tassis in London that he was to warn the Earl of Nottingham that any "scandal" in matters of worship in his embassy would be considered a violation of the new treaty.[28] The dispatch reached London after Howard's departure.

As events turned out, the forebodings of the Council about this question were quite pointless. The two Protestant chaplains of the Embassy, Wadsworth and Palmer, were quite unlike the tactless Doctor Man. In fact, later in September, Wadsworth became a Catholic during a visit to Salamanca to the extreme annoy-ance of Sir Charles Cornwallis.[29] The English embassy was a great success throughout Howard's stay in Spain; there is a note of true satisfaction in his secret report to Cecil of April 28, "I must say to your Lordship that in all my life I never saw soe kinde a people of all sortes."[30] For the two months of Howard's visit there were many great spectacles presented to please the English visitors: pageants, bull fights, masques, tournaments and banquets. There were also three magnificent religious ceremonies at the Court which were well noted in all accounts of this embassy: the solemn ratification of the treaty, the christening of the young heir to the Spanish throne, the future Philip IV, and the famous procession for the feast of *Corpus Christi* beginning at the towering, but unfinished, façade of the Cathedral of Valladolid. In the latter ceremony some of Howard's retinue marched to the great interest of the Spanish Court and especially to one of King Philip's confidants on English affairs, the Jesuit, Joseph Creswell.[31]

Although he had left England twenty-five years before, Creswell by virtue of his office as agent for the English colleges in Spain was most anxious to learn of the Earl of Nottingham's attitude on religious affairs. Three of his private letters give considerable information how Charles Howard handled this delicate question during his visit. Since the ambassador's letters to Robert Cecil and Treswell's *Relation* are silent on this topic, Creswell's letters fill in an important lacuna.

Creswell and Nottingham had a long interview on April 1, Easter Monday, which he immediately summarized in a private report for the Duke of Lerma. He stated that Howard had received him in his palace with great cordiality "and embraced me as his son." The two men then paced up and down the gallery for half an hour under the gaze of Howard's retinue after which, while the elderly Nottingham rested in a chair, Creswell "adduced his reasons in favor of the Catholics and of the peace without entering into theology to his great pleasure and of those standing by." Creswell said the English College in Valladolid—one of the colleges so thoroughly denounced in Parliament when the recusancy laws were confirmed in the previous year— would be honored if Howard would visit it. Howard appeared to be quite pleased with Creswell, for after summoning his herald he presented the English Jesuit with a copy of his coat of arms and titles and observed that he hoped his visit would be the beginning of great union and good to both countries. He solemnly promised that "as he had done his duty in time of war so now would he defend the peace with his life and sword."[32]

The visit of the Earl of Nottingham to the English College was a diplomatic triumph. After he saw the small courtyard and red brick buildings he addressed

[27] E 2557/30.
[28] E 2512/3–4.
[29] J. W. Stoye, *English Travelers Abroad*, pp. 338 ff.
[30] S.P. 94/11/45.
[31] See Stoye, pp. 332 ff.; E 2557/38.
[32] E 2557/40.

the students in English and expressed his pleasure at the splendor of the religious service of thanksgiving after the ratification of the treaty. He greeted each of the students and reminded them that they were "of his nation" and expressed the hope that some day he would see King James grant liberty of conscience. He especially noted the example of Henry IV in France offering toleration to two religions in an obvious reference to Philip's difficulties in the Low Countries.[33]

In this indirect fashion, as Howard knew that his remarks would be reported to the Spanish Court, the position of this powerful English Councilor was made clear. He was in favor of toleration and hoped that it would be granted some day. He showed by his courtesy to Creswell and the students of the college that he did not believe the typical Puritan rumors against them, but there were no rash offers of help. He was clearly in favor of the peace and was anxious to keep King James in the same frame of mind, which was not going to be a difficult task. Despite the contagious atmosphere of cordiality, Howard had not promised any significant change in James' policy, yet he had avoided direct embarrassment to the Spanish Court.

While Charles Howard was performing this diplomatic mission with considerable skill, some of his entourage began to make more open overtures to Spain. Creswell reported to the Duke of Lerma and the Council of State that "various gentlemen and captains of the ships in the service of the late queen in the embassy of the Admiral" had expressed a desire to enter Philip's service either in the Spanish navy or armies in Flanders. Their reason is a partial explanation of the occasional participation of some of Howard's retinue in the Catholic services in Spain: "they have been persuaded by their Catholic relatives that, for their honour and the relief of their consciences, it would be better to serve his Majesty and die—should it be necessary—in a just war than under the standard of disloyal rebels." The request was not a new one at the Spanish court; there had been a regular trickle of Catholics to the Low Countries, and to Spain during the war and from various records it is clear that well over a hundred had become regular Spanish pensioners in their exile.[34]

After considering this request, Philip III and his Council decided not to alter their usual practice in treating these cases, which was that each petitioner should draw up a brief memorial and have it considered for a possible recommendation to the Archduke. The noteworthy thing in this memorandum of Creswell is that it reflects an obvious secrecy among the English retinue of Howard. He was certainly convinced that they were sincere, for he said that they came to visit him "as Nicodemus in the night to protect themselves from spies." Cornwallis, who was preparing to assume his post as resident ambassador, was quite unaware of it. At nearly the same time he reported that the English Catholic refugees at Valladolid, noticing "the conjunction of amities" between England and Spain, were sure that Philip would show "more coldness both in affection and liberalitie than heretofore."[35] Similarly, Treswell in his *Relation* gave no indication that a number of the military men in the Howard retinue offered to remain in Spain. It is more likely that many of them would later offer to join in England the regiment soon to be recruited by Arundel on behalf of the Archduke.

Finally, with both countries satisfied that due honor had been shown with lavish pageantry and attention to protocol, it was time for Howard's visit to come to an end. He had been on Spanish soil for over ten weeks; he had even traveled to Madrid to visit his cousin, Jane Dormer, the Duchess of Feria, whose son was then Viceroy of Sicily. The laconic diarist recorded their departure as follows: "The nineteenth day of June his Lordship came on board the *Beare* to goe into England, out of the town of Saint Danderos [Santander] and the twentieth day he set saile from thence in the afternoone, the next day being Friday we lost the sight of Spaine."[36]

Even as Howard's squadron headed northward to England Juan de Tassis received an order to prepare to return to Spain as his successor, Pedro de Zúñiga, would arrive in a few weeks with new instructions. Tassis was unwell; there had been occasional remarks in his dispatches during the spring hinting that a successor would soon be needed. The new envoy reached England in mid-July. Zúñiga reported to Philip III after Tassis' departure that he would continue to pay the pensions for English courtiers that had been already arranged. He also reported that he was advised of the plan to buy some measure of toleration for Catholics. He gave no details; the cryptic phrasing implied that he would see for himself.[37]

With the departure of Juan de Tassis, the Count of Villa Mediana, the Spanish embassy in England lost the leadership of a man of dogged determination, which had not been blunted by the frustrating turn of events during the past two years. Philip's over-ambitious insistence on the priority of toleration had been faithfully and prudently served. Yet it had come to nothing. In the summer of 1605 there was a silence in Zúñiga's dispatches on the subject, for King James was pushing on with his own inflexible policy. A proclamation was even sent to the Catholics of Ireland: it regretted that "rumours of an intended toleration of religion and liberty of conscience have been spread. The Law will be strictly enforced in Ireland as elsewhere."[38] It appeared as if nothing could be done.

[33] A.R.S.J. Anglia 36, ff. 235–236, 237–238v, Report to Acquaviva, Italian. April, 1605.

[34] E 2557/41. A. J. Loomie, *The Spanish Elizabethans*, chapter five, and appendix.

[35] E 2557/38, *Winwood Memorials* 2: p. 72.

[36] *The Royal Entertainment* . . . , p. 21.

[37] E. 2584/47.

[38] *Tudor and Stuart Proclamations* 2: no. 182.

It was only seven weeks after Howard's departure that the Count of Villa Mediana finally reached the Spanish Court. He was a sickly man and, there is little doubt, he was a disappointed man. Cornwallis, who had not the slightest knowledge of what a difficult task Tassis had undertaken in England, could only remark with a certain spitefulness on the former ambassador's reception at Valladolid:

> Very certain it is that there is here had a great distaste of the Conde de Villa Medina (*sic*). . . . This they are contented secretely to deliver that as long as he was imployed only in the office of courtier and to make love to us he performed very well his parte, but after he entered into negotiation he hath shewed himself to be out of his element and made much demonstration of his weakness.[39]

While Cornwallis was prone to believe rumors without much scrutiny, it is apparent that Tassis had become a scapegoat for Spain's failure to secure the peace most suitable to the objections of Philip III. Tassis was too unwell to defend himself, and his silence served to quiet a fruitless exchange of recriminations. Early in 1607 the Count of Villa Mediana died and his body was interred in the floor of the chapel of the Augustinian convent at Valladolid.

VI. THE PERSPECTIVE OF HISTORY

From its origins to its outcome the trail of the secret diplomacy of Don Juan de Tassis has been traced through scattered dispatches, *consultas,* and private letters. There remain, however, some basic questions to discuss. What is the place within the "Counter Reform" era of these diplomatic designs of Spain? In the analysis of this Spanish failure is there any clue to the later momentous decline of its hegemony? What could have been done by Philip III to avoid such a sterile and disheartening outcome for his English policy? Did the Hapsburgs abandon the notion of intervening on behalf of the English Catholics, or were there any similar attempts later? What were the results within English history of this diplomatic maneuver?

Undoubtedly this hitherto little-known diplomatic intrigue is quite relevant to the growing conviction of diplomatic historians that the influence of religion on the formation of policy at this period can be easily misunderstood, or exaggerated.[1] The older, more enduring elements of geography, economics, and the internal politics of nations still exerted a sovereign determination on the foreign policies of the western monarchies. The "Reform" and the "Counter Reform" introduced religious slogans which added a new element of propaganda to mask the unchanging pursuit of national self-interest. For the efforts of Juan de Tassis and the Constable of Castile to negotiate a ticklish issue, such

as toleration, amid the more predictable agenda after a cease fire were stalled and then eventually abandoned. It should not be a surprise that religion was submerged by the more enduring issues of sixteenth-century diplomacy; it would have been unusual if it did not. The paradox of the incident is that in an era where the calculations of the diplomat tended, in performance, to lip service for religion, the King of the wealthiest monarchy of western Europe acted as if he were unaware of the contemporary scene.

A solicitude about the treatment of another ruler's subjects, so earnest that it could become a protracted diplomatic negotiation, is a rarity in European history. In the nineteenth century the Near Eastern rivalry of France and Russia clashed over an analogous problem; yet there were motives of personal prestige and national influence also at stake. Philip, using the panoply of Hapsburg power exclusively, had proved an unsubtle advocate on behalf of the English Catholics. Yet success would have increased his stature within Spain, and the many assurances of his father to the Catholics would have been at last redeemed. In such an event the complaints of the Spanish clergy over his father's disengagement from the nation's historic war with the Turk in the Mediterranean would be silenced. For, beginning with a truce in March, 1577, and concluding with a peace in 1581, Philip had altered the historic policy for his kingdom against Islam.[2]

In London, Don Juan de Tassis was, in certain respects, renewing a crusade. A historian of the last generation has viewed the year 1581 as the apogee of Spanish grandeur. After this time, since Spain was "bereft of the ancient inspiration of crusading, she ceased to go forward and began to go back."[3] Undoubtedly, there was a heady persuasion working in the back of Philip's mind of a return to a crusading tradition. This was deep in the living memory of his subjects. Yet Professor Merriman's observation, while stimulating, is not as enlightening as it may at first appear. Historically, Spain's sixteenth-century grandeur was not due simply to its aggressive pursuit of a holy war, it was owed rather to other factors: advantageous marriage alliances, the temporary eclipse of its rivals, and an astute use of its resources of manpower and wealth either against the Turks on the sea, or the Valois in Italy. The policy of Philip in 1603 was not in the tradition of Spanish greatness precisely because it was begun without a sufficiently careful appraisal of the odds to be faced. Nor was there a proper assessment of Spain's resources to accomplish the elusive task before it. The decline of Spain can be traced more clearly in subsequent decades in similar miscalculations on a far more grandiose and disastrously expensive scale.

Yet Philip III would soon be denounced by a power-

---

[39] *Winwood, Memorials* **2**: p. 109.

[1] See G. Zeller, *Les Temps Modernes,* pp. 122–128, in P. Renouvin, ed., *Histoire des Relations Internationales,* tome II.

[2] Braudel, *op. cit.,* pp. 996, 1006.

[3] R. B. Merriman, *The Rise of the Spanish Empire* **4**: p. 155.

ful Spanish ecclesiastic who viewed the treaty of London as an "appeasement" of England. In March, 1608, the aging but still incisive Juan de Rivera, the Archbishop of Valencia, and since 1602 the Viceroy of the kingdom, addressed an angry letter to the Council of State. He was exercised over the influence which the English merchants residing in his city were having over his flock. He felt they were giving bad example by living openly "in their sect." The treaty was responsible for this relaxed situation, he charged, whereas in England the lot of the Catholics was still to be deplored. He demanded to know why Spain in 1604 had not in fact lived up to its greatness, but instead had abandoned a just war. The Council, through Don Juan de Idiaquez, defended its previous conduct:

The Constable's journey to England was principally to se-cure a favorable change in the question of religion. This was his Majesty's intention, and it was performed in a way that was licit and suitable, he is confident that God, who judges by the intention, shall accept what occured. A negotiation can be well begun and still be overturned.[4]

Was this explanation, while intended only to quiet the angry prelate, an adequate one? From the point of view of Idiaquez and Philip it was. For the dexterity to withdraw from the well-established prejudices and impressive suspicions against forming an *entente* with France and the Papacy was unknown at the court of the Spanish Hapsburgs. Yet the quest of toleration would have been more likely to succeed if the difficult task of reaching a full understanding with Pope Clement and Henry IV had been first pursued. Philip III was deprived of both the support and the advice of other Catholic princes. The Papacy did not have much op-portunity to appreciate what Spain's policy implied, for Sessa was not able to explain the reasons for its adoption. Even the envoys of the Archduke were not encouraged by Spain to assist in the delicate task, al-though their instructions from Brussels allowed them to do so. In fact by the end of 1604 the estrangement had reached the level of having the Council of State debate the possibility of asking the Archduke to con-sider the post of Viceroy of Sicily.[5]

Jean Richardot had pointed out the indifference of Spain to the views of Brussels at the end of the confer-ence, by explaining that in the Spanish commissioners, "they did not have companions, but masters." [6]

The wisdom of placing toleration as the first point of diplomatic business, when it could be postponed, might also be debated. However, in the long run, this differ-ence over timing was not impressive. King James and Parliament had been no more in agreement on the Catholic question early in 1604 than they were a year later. Yet Philip was stubborn on this point. Pre-

viously in June, 1601, when the feasibility of a Catho-lic candidacy for the English throne was being ex-plored, he warned that the religious issue had to retain priority: ". . . since all the reasons which maintain me, and the realms which God has given me, depend on it." [7] The line between the crusade and the *raison d'état* had become blurred. Philip, in spite of his claims of disinterestedness, had insisted upon a personal theory as the only basis for a satisfactory peace.

It has long been recognized that during these early years of the reign of James I the great issues of religion, economics, and politics, which were to lead to the impassioned struggles of the 1640's, were begin-ning to emerge. The secret negotiations of Spain from 1603 to 1605 have highlighted at least one of these fundamental problems. King James, apparently, looked upon the Catholics as a danger of the future, not the present.

In his speech at the opening of the first Parliament of his reign the King observed that it were best to leave their present status unaltered. He felt impelled to issue a clear warning:

But of one thing would I have the Papists of this land to be admonished: that they presume not too much upon my lenity . . . as therupon to increase their number and strength in this kingdom: whereby if not in my time at least in the time of my posterity they might be in hope to erect their religion again.[8]

Prior to expressing these sentiments James had allowed a large part of the fines to be remitted as a token of his tolerant inclinations.

Yet at this occasion, when James intended to deal with the recusant problem on his own, the Puritan will in Parliament prevailed. At the very moment that a substantial mitigation—if not a total abrogation—of the recusancy laws was under serious secret discussion among some of the Privy Council, Parliament renewed the full code of laws against Catholics. James was re-duced to the shabby expedient of privately assuring the foreign ambassadors that he did not really intend to enforce them. It is true that some of the courtiers in-volved in the secret plan were venal, and even hopeful of some spoils from Spain in the very midst of the negotiations, but their efforts were spurred by self-inter-est. The outcome of the toleration intrigue in the summer of 1604 was an indication that the decision in this matter no longer rested with the Crown and its advisers. The opponents of toleration were formidable in Parliament: there were Puritans in the Commons and the Anglican bishops in the Lords. It was sig-nificant that Robert Cecil, the most influential adviser of James, even though he understood the meaning of James's appeasing gestures towards Catholics, could not be won, even by bribes, to support toleration. Parlia-ment insisted on its jealously guarded right to enact

[4] P. Boronat y Barrachina, *Los Moriscos y su Expulsion* 2: p. 121 note 9.

[5] Lonchay and Cuvelier 1: pp. 205–206.

[6] P.E.A. liv 364 f. 220 v.

[7] E 2023/48.

[8] *Commons Journal* 1: p. 144.

and repeal legislation and it reacted nervously to the slightest effort of the Crown to mitigate the original repressive intent of the recusancy laws. The initiative was safely with Parliament, for there would never be an effective toleration without a proper legal enactment.

In bribing some of the English Privy Council to look favorably on the Catholics Juan de Tassis and Philip were deceived. These courtiers did not have the power to grant toleration, at best they could interfere in the administration of the recusancy laws in individual cases of clients and friends. Some of the Spanish Council of State—Juan de Idiaquez especially—grasped this insufficiency in the diplomacy pursued by Tassis. They questioned the wisdom of negotiating in secret for what was really a matter of public policy. They shrewdly insisted that any payments by Spain should be preceded by a public proclamation guaranteeing the promised mitigation of laws. They stipulated carefully—although in the actual events they were ignored—that a pension was to be given only in so far as the desired effect was attained. In the end the Count of Villa Mediana was revealed to be negotiating simply with the few friendly courtiers who would help him when and if the risk was not great. In some instances there was sincerity, but there was also little strength by comparison with what the opposition could and did muster.

After Juan de Tassis had been in England for five weeks he had in effect predicted to Philip III that toleration was not possible but he was instructed to continue. As a result the envoy did what he could, he attempted to build a clique of courtiers to assist a secret negotiation. It would be difficult to expect Juan de Tassis to appreciate rapidly the English political situation. King James had made many secret and misleading protestations of his desire to change the lot of the Catholics of England. These statements were believed for a time by many English Catholics, Pope Clement VIII, and most of all by Philip III. James's true sentiments were revealed in his secret correspondence to Sir Robert Cecil before his accession. That the sincerity of James can be questioned, is really beside the point. The consequences of these secret protestations were historically significant for they were in fact believed. Philip III labored under the misapprehension that James was sincere and also capable of taking the initiative and having his way, as Philip could in fact do in Spain. The unequal contest was over in two years. It was a true miniature of further and larger struggles that were to come between Crown and Parliament in the next decades. The power to determine the fate of the Catholics was never to be in the hands of King James.

It is equally useful to outline the tenuous beginnings of the "Spanish Faction" of later years. Robert Cecil was a pensioner of Spain but hardly its devoted friend. He retained his pro-Dutch sympathies of the past, and remained consistently unencouraging over toleration.

The Howards, as on other occasions, presented varying attitudes during these two years. It was their close friendship with Cecil that really gave importance to their activities. The Earl of Northampton and the Countess of Suffolk emerged as the most active pro-Spanish courtiers. The Earl of Suffolk and the Earl of Nottingham appeared friendly to Spain, but hardly partisan. Lord Buckhurst, whatever his tolerant inclinations, was not outspoken on the question. Several Scottish nobles in the "faction," though friendly to Spain—and in the event far more than had been expected—were ill at ease with their English rivals. Thus, in the first testing, the "Spanish faction" was indecisive and uncoordinated. In its first years it appears as an amorphous clique without a leading and reflective personality at its head. The result was that Spain's policy had an unreliable foundation at the English court.

The selection of Don Juan de Tassis as the envoy for a truly auspicious mission may also be questioned. The Constable of Castile had no reservations in complaining that Tassis was not of the first rank among ambassadors in Spanish service. Yet criticism from that source can be properly suspected since he was anxious to receive the post, and his own intransigent attitude towards the Papacy was not a good credential in any case. King Philip, as in other aspects of this negotiation, did not trouble to explain his personal decisions. In the absolutist Hapsburg tradition, the choice was simply another instance of *"stet pro ratione voluntas."* Yet it would not be out of place to note that one of the most significant treaties in Spanish history, the peace with the Sublime Porte of 1581, had been handled with unexpected success by the unknown Giovanni Margliani.[9]

There can be an interesting, if tangential, speculation about the diplomatic skill of someone as knowledgeable as Don Juan de Idiaquez, who as secretary to Philip II and Philip III, had become one of the best-informed courtiers about English affairs. Similarly the able Don Baltazar de Zúñiga was not chosen. Later his talents were to be fully employed in his famous embassy at the court of the Holy Roman Empire. Clearly the choice of Tassis was part of the pattern of Philip's handling of policy. He did not understand England, nor did he see what diplomatic steps would have a chance of success. However, considering the opposition in England, at the time of James's accession, to the Spanish objectives, it can be reasonably assumed that the history of this diplomatic intervention would not be substantially altered even in the hands of the gifted Gondomar.

It is interesting to survey the later developments which can be traced to a treaty which displeased Philip so much at first. The reign of peace between the kingdoms, the relief from the expensive defenses against English privateers, even the longevity of the "Spanish

---

[9] Braudel, *op. cit.,* pp. 993 ff.

faction" at the English court were not to be appreciated until later. For at the outset there were still to be too many reports of seizures of English cargoes under the charge that they were destined for the enemies of Spain. Moreover, there was to be a considerable amount of expensive and protracted litigation by English merchants over cargoes confiscated during the war. Even a secret protocol of the treaty [10] regulating the Inquisition's activity was to have only a limited success, for many complaints were to appear in the dispatches of the English envoys, Sir Charles Cornwallis and Sir John Digby.

It will hardly be a surprise that the treaty, though applauded in the city of London, was never really popular in other parts of England, where the denunciations were vehement enough to be noted by the Venetian ambassador several years later.[11] Moreover, there lingered a popular misconception that England had flourished because of the war, whereas, in fact, prosperity had come only to certain individuals while the Crown's debts had soared. A second illusion had been that the interests of the United Provinces could never be in rivalry with England. It was after the truce of 1609 in the Low Countries that Dutch aggressiveness —dramatically illustrated in the massacre of Englishmen at Amboyna—was to begin to dull the long-lived sympathy for their cause in England. By 1617 King James was able finally to negotiate the English withdrawal from the cautionary towns. His instructions for his ambassador on this occasion noted that England would never have the right to claim them as her own, that the garrisons were costly to maintain, and thus it was best to surrender them under fair conditions.[12]

Although the relations between London and Brussels were more friendly in the aftermath of the treaty there was one serious crisis which involved the religious issue dramatically. The Archduke Albert had been the protector for many English Catholic refugees during the war and continued to help them later. However, in the aftermath and furor of the "Gunpowder Plot" of November, 1605, charges of conspiracy were lodged against two prominent refugees: Hugh Owen and Father William Baldwin. The English ambassador demanded their immediate arrest and deportation in chains to England to stand trial. At first the Archduke placed Owen under house arrest, but soon after, with the strong encouragement of Philip III, he announced that sufficient evidence was not being offered by the English envoy to warrant sending either of the accused to England. In London, however, the Archduke's envoy, Baron Hoboken, was summoned to the presence of King James on several occasions to hear impassioned complaints over the Archduke's unfriendliness in this

matter. The crisis was prolonged into later in the spring of 1606 during which time the controversy widened to include the Catholic attitude to the proposed oath of allegiance in England. Robert Cecil had frequent interviews with the young ambassador from Brussels in which he complained about the Archduke's subservience to Philip III. At one point Cecil startled Hoboken by offering to settle all outstanding difficulties with the Archduke while promising in return some measure of toleration for the English Catholics. In exchange the Archduke was to represent to the Papacy that it should announce explicitly that it would never seek to depose King James. The Archduke and his principal adviser, Jean Richardot, countered with the proposal that a discussion of the differences between the courts of England and Brussels would be sincere when the alliance with the Dutch had been ended.[13] Cecil angrily withdrew the offer of toleration and the matter rested there. Owens and Baldwin continued to be under the Archduke's protection.

A year after the Truce of 1609 the Archduke made a cautious inquiry with his envoy in London as to whether there was any chance that he might do something on behalf of the Catholics of England. Louis de Groote, the successor to Hoboken, replied on September 10 that the situation was far too delicate for any such intervention. "Any attempt by Your Highness, as well as by the King of Spain, will always be insulting to the King and his Council. For they consider the problem in the light that the Catholics have no other support but the Hapsburgs." He warned that foreign interference would probably hurt the Catholics rather than help them and concluded that even if King James would want to be lenient to Catholics "he will be turned away and prevented by Parliament which will not allow it." [14]

The report that, in the spring of 1606, Robert Cecil had discussed the possibility of toleration with Hoboken —although it had obviously been only part of a diplomatic gambit—came to the attention of Salisbury's close friend, the Earl of Suffolk. Waiting for an opportune moment, Suffolk made a very guarded offer to revive the earlier negotiations on recusancy fines, which had been abandoned eighteen months before during the last weeks of the embassy of Juan de Tassis. While the pattern of the offer was the same as the former, all the figures in this new secret plan were different. They were now to be Father Henry Blount, the successor to Father Henry Garnet as Superior of the Jesuits in England; William Howard of Naworth Castle, the brother of Suffolk; and Pedro de Zúñiga, who had learned of the former intrigue from Tassis. It was to be Zúñiga's first experience of that tantalizing and elusive prospect that Spain might still be of some help to the Catholics.

William Howard was a Catholic who shunned the

---

[10] The official copy of Philip's ratification was sent to Brussels on June 15, 1605. A.G.R. P.E.A. liv. 364 f. 299.

[11] Cal. S.P. Venetian 11: p. 6; 12: p. 231. See also *Winwood, Memorials* 2: p. 217.

[12] Folger Library MS. V.b. 239 ff. 154–60, copies.

[13] *Revue de Histoire Ecclesiastique* 8 (1907): 91–96.

[14] P.E.A. liv. 365 ff. 313–313 v.

life of the Court and devoted himself to his library and his large estates near the Scottish border where he was affectionately respected.[15] In December, 1606, according to Blount's private report to Robert Persons, Suffolk was encouraging Lord William to approach Pedro de Zúñiga for a large bribe, "promising faithfully that some good shall be done for the Catholics." It was as vague an offer as any that Tassis had received. Blount was reserved about the success of the secret offer, for he noticed that Suffolk obviously had other motives. "Salisbury will resist: yet such is the want of money with the Chamberlain [Suffolk] at this time . . . that either Salisbury must supply or else he must needs break with him and trust to this refuge." [16] Since Cecil's hostile attitude to toleration was unchanged it would appear that Suffolk's new foray into the Catholic question was largely a cynical attempt to force Salisbury to help him financially. When Robert Persons reported the secret offer to Pope Paul V, he clearly suspected that the plan had very shaky foundations:

I have my suspicions of this business as to whether the Councilors wish only to extract money and to let the Catholics down. However it seems to me that it will not be a bad thing to entertain the project until we see what security they are going to give.[17]

Since no security was given, this small scale renewal of the early intensive negotiations of Tassis came to nothing.

A different variation on the experiences of Tassis was to occur five years later. The scheme was that Catholics would pay a general fine and then be left free to worship "in their houses." At this time James was even more desperately in need of revenue than in the summer of 1604. In February, 1611, the final session of the first Jacobean Parliament had closed with the urgent question of the royal finances still unsolved after the promising solution of the "Great Contract" had foundered in mutual suspicions. A year later a special and urgent dispatch reached Brussels which was copied and sent to Madrid. It stated that Sir Thomas Lake, the King's Secretary, had approached the leaders of the English Catholics, with King James' approval, offering them immunity from all prosecution in return for an unspecified sum of money.[18]

Although the negotiations for "the Spanish marriage" had been figuring for the past months in the dispatches of Alonso de Velasco, the new Spanish ambassador, Lake's maneuvre was made apparently without any direct reference to Spain. The report stated that the known "inclination of a greater part of the Council" gave Lake's offer considerable authority. At least the

condition of the royal treasury would certainly give it credibility. However, the report stressed the many complexities that were involved in collecting such a common fine, or "composition." The greatest obstacle was Lake's intention to place "the most important families" under obligation for the entire fine when it was finally agreed upon. This was quite dangerous for the few hapless Catholics selected as surety to the Crown for the payments of others. It implied that they would be dunning the rest for their share, and surely would lead to intolerable tensions. It was also noted that the plan would end the safe obscurity of many Catholics unknown to the recusant rolls: "at present they are passing over many who pay nothing for they are not discovered, and they are afraid of the Treasurer's hand."

These practical difficulties apparently proved too heavy to allow the plan to be discussed further. King James would instead have to rely upon his traditional sources of revenue. The bitter rebuff of the "Addled Parliament" of two years later was still awaiting him.

For several years after the treaty Spain continued its policy of pensions to a small list of courtiers in England. Slowly, and only after the death of Robert Cecil, King James began to seek a stronger alliance with Spain. His motives were largely a fear of isolation, since the pro-Spanish policy of Marie de Medici, as regent for her son Louis XIII, led James to fear that England, disenchanted with the Dutch and in a poor second place —after Spain—in French policy, would now be without friends. According to a Catholic Scottish noble at Court, Sarmiento reported to Spain, it was Cecil's insistence in 1611 that England must still try to form an anti-Spanish league that finally led James to dismiss him.[19] Shortly after this Robert Cecil died, and the most powerful critic of the Spanish faction passed from the scene.

Diego de Sarmiento's dispatches for the year 1614 reflect these changes with great clarity. Of the four resident Spanish ambassadors who had known James up to this time, his estimate of the King was by far the most favorable. Sarmiento reported that he had found James to be sincere, open minded, peace loving, and even anxious to alleviate the condition of the Catholics were it not for the opposition of the Puritans.[20] It was an easy excuse to blame the Puritans for everything, but Sarmiento evidently agreed with James' excuses, and that only increased their friendship.

By November, 1617, Sarmiento—now Count of Gondomar—was so very certain of James' deep friendship for Spain that he even advised Philip III to discontinue the original plan of Tassis of pensions for English courtiers. The aged Lord Howard of Effingham and Robert Carr, Earl of Somerset, then headed the list with the Countess of Suffolk also receiving a sizable

[15] See G. Ormsby, "The Household Books of Lord William Howard of Naworth Castle," *The Surtees Society* **68**, introduction.

[16] Stonyhurst MS. Anglia A–III f. 72.

[17] A.S.V. Fondo Borghese II **448** ab f. 332.

[18] E 627/49. *Avisos* 16 February, 1612.

[19] *Documentos Inéditos* **3**: pp. 156–160; letter of 16 November, 1613.

[20] *Ibid.* **3**: pp. 56–60, 208–210; **4**: pp. 111–112.

pension. Sir Thomas Lake, Sir William Monson, and Lady Drummond were accepting regular payments as well. However, Gondomar no longer looked on these courtiers as important informants. He believed that any clever ambassador could acquire their advice at much less expense by the ordinary gifts and courtesies of his office. He told Philip frankly that the pensions were largely wasted and it would be better to give the money to the English colleges in Spain—there were four at that time—or to build up the Spanish navy.[21] Philip was reluctant to withdraw his pensions abruptly. He hesitated, perhaps, because as even Gondomar admitted, both the United Provinces and France were spending more money than Spain in bribes at the English Court.

The path of Sarmiento's steady success had been smoothed by James' persistent hopes for a Spanish marriage for his heir Prince Charles. The King's motives were centered on the large dowry of the bride, as well as a useful alliance as a counterpoise to France. Yet as early as 1615 he secretly promised the nonenforcement of the recusancy laws as part of a marriage treaty with Spain. His opportunistic concession was, of course, premature. The protracted tensions over Raleigh's illegal invasion of the Orinoco, followed by the mounting resentment of the Puritans over the Hapsburg success in Bohemia were to make such a marriage too unpopular. By the autumn of 1621 the "Great Protestation" of the House of Commons, among other points, denounced "Popery" and Spain. It was a blatant sign that the Commons' dislike of toleration for Catholics was as adamant as ever. Yet James' impatient dismissal of Parliament in 1622 would leave him with no alternative, but Gondomar's diplomacy.

In a sense, the Spanish envoy had been too successful. Early in 1623 to the embarrassed surprise of both courts, Prince Charles set off for Madrid to begin his courtship of the Infanta Maria. Were it not for this naïve and expensive junket, King James would not have been forced for the first time to offer a solid proof of his tolerant inclinations. Nearly two decades after Don Juan de Tassis had first begun to negotiate for toleration James actually drafted, in the summer of 1623, a pardon for all recusants to be obtained by their payment of a nominal fee.[22]

This royal pardon, once the goal of so much sustained diplomatic intrigue, proved to be an illusion. In the autumn of 1623 the whole marriage negotiation, like any pile of dead leaves, was swiftly blown apart by mutual suspicions. Prince Charles turned to France. However, the insistence of Cardinal Richelieu that the marriage treaty on behalf of Henriette-Marie was to contain the same liberties for English Catholics, as Spain had secured, was to be equally barren of results. Despite a flourish of royal pledges, proclamations and pardons, numerous justices continued to sentence recusants at the assizes.[23]

James's reign was to close with the anti-Spanish sentiment of the country approving a war which was to be conducted with the same lack of realistic leadership and caution that had previously made the marriage diplomacy futile. When peace with Spain was finally agreed upon, the treaty was to be little more than a renewal of the terms so laboriously negotiated twenty-six years before in London. The reason, from Spain's point of view, was phrased sententiously on August 20, 1630, in the Council of State's advice to Philip IV: "The state of things has not provided an opening for a change." Once again the possibility of securing an article on toleration was debated in Spain. This time the Count of Oñate and the Marquis of Floresdavila formulated the deciding opinion. "Although in the former treaty the point of religion was omitted," they wrote, "as well as in this one, there were then presented particular reasons to cease insisting upon it. According to the opinion of the religious and experienced people of the kingdom of England this had been to the greater benefit of the Catholics." Therefore, they advised King Philip IV that, although the point had been dropped again, "it should not be so passed over in silence that the English envoy would believe that your Majesty has forgotten his obligation, or that there was some matter of state in this silence." They advised that a draft article on toleration should be submitted to England simply as a demonstration of concern, but without any hope of success.[24]

This was done and, not unexpectedly, it was soon set aside. The crisis of the Swedish intervention in the Holy Roman Empire was already far advanced, and Spain's attention could not be diverted to English Catholic affairs. Moreover, Charles I was secretly promising the Spanish envoy in London a force of 12,000 men. This too, was a useless gesture, since in fact he could not afford to help.

Later, however, when Charles' troubles mounted in Scotland with the opening of the "Bishops' War" in 1637 the pattern of events had come full turn. The King of England was discussing in secret the hiring of Spanish veteran troops to join his standard. It was a fruitless plan. Yet the desperate search for expedients never ceased with that hard pressed Stuart monarch. Two years later, in 1639, the Catholics of England as a group were asked to make a common collection of money to buttress the shaky finances of the Crown.

These efforts, which were probably an amplification of the pattern of secret inquiries of the second year of Tassis' embassy in England, had an unusual origin. As the disaster in Scotland became more evident, Queen Henriette-Marie begged the leaders of the Catholics to

[21] Ibid. 1: p. 131.

[22] Cal. S.P. Dom. 1623–1625, p. 73. D. H. Willson, King James VI and I, pp. 366–368, 431 ff.

[23] M. J. Havran, The Catholics in Caroline England (Stanford, 1962), pp. 18 ff.

[24] E 2519/103, consulta of 20 August, 1630.

SOURCES

MANUSCRIPTS

I. SPAIN
Archivo General de Simancas
Sección de Estado
Legajos 840–843. The principal series of diplomatic dispatches and correspondence on English Affairs, 1602–1605. Legajos 2512–2514, 2584, to 2588, 2557 and 2571 are an invaluable supplement to the former series containing many of the consultas of the Council and drafts of dispatches. Legajos 618 to 625. The principal diplomatic series between Brussels and the Spanish court containing several important original dispatches on England. Legajos 2023–2024, 2224, 2288–89 are the supplementary series of consultas, etc. Legajos 973, 975, 977, 1855–1856 and K 1602 to 1607, letters from the Roman embassy and about French affairs.

Saint Alban's College Archive (Valladolid)
Miscellaneous Papers: Legajos 1, 13, 16
San Lucar Papers: Legajos 1 and 2B/655

Archivo Historico Nacional
Sección de Estado
Libros 250–266, 292–295. Copies of the executive orders of the Council of State, several pertaining to the question of the English trading in Spain.

Biblioteca Nacional
MS. 2347 ff. 210–227, contemporary copy of the "Relacion de la Yda del Condestable de Castilla."

II. ENGLAND
British Museum
Sloane MS. 1851, "A Short Diary of the Conference and Proceedings in the Treatie of London 1604" (Copies also in Add. MS. 14033 and Add. MS. 35, 847)
Egerton MS. 1507, 1508

Public Record Office
S.P. 14, vols. 1–14
S.P. 94, vols. 1–11

Westminster Cathedral Archive
Series A, vols. 1–7
Series E, vol. 2 (The Papers of Thomas Fitzherbert)

Stonyhurst College
"Collectanea Patris Greene" vols. B. M. P
Anglia MS. vol. 3

Maritime Museum, Greenwich
Philip MS. vol. 91 and Welcome MS. vol. 6 (Miscellaneous papers concerning Spanish affairs)

III. ITALY
Archivio Segredo di Vaticano
Nunziatura di Spagna vols. 40–54 and 320–323
Fondo Borghese vol. II 448 AB

Archive of the Society of Jesus (Rome)
Hispania, Epistolae Receptae vols. 135–140.
Anglia, vols. 30 and 31 (in two parts).

IV. BELGIUM
Archives Générales du Royaume
Papiers d'Etats et d'Audience, livres 360–369.

V. THE UNITED STATES
Folger Library
V.b. 142, contemporary copy of the articles of the treaty.
V.b. 239, State Papers, copies.
V.b. 321, State Papers, copies.
G.a. 1 and 8, Political and religious tracts, copies.
X. d. 322, The petition of the "Lay Catholics" of England, copy.

CONTEMPORARY BOOKS

ANON. n.d. *La Segunda Parte de la Embaxada de Don Juan de Tassis, Conde de Villa Mediana, Embaxador de su Magestad real del Rey don Felipe Tercero nuestro Señor para el nuevo Rey Jacobo de Inglaterra: Da se cuenta de lo que su Magestad le respondio y los grandes comedimientos que se le hizieron.* Lisbon.

ANON. 1585. *A True Report of the General Embarrement of all the English Shippes, under the dom(inion) of the Kinge of Spaine: and of the daungerous adventures and wonderful deliverance of a ship of London called the Violet being of the burden of 130 tonne: by the special pro(vidence) of God from the violence of Spanyards at a port called Sebastian in Biskay: which adventure was enterprised 25 of May 1585 and was finished the 29 of the same month without hurt to either men or ship.* London.

ANON. 1604. *The Supplication of certaine Masse Priests falsely called Catholikes Directed to the Kings most excellent Maiestie, now this time of Parliament, but scattered in corners to moue malcontents to Mutinie. Published with a marginal glosse and an answer to the Libellers reasons againe renewed and augmented and by Sections applied to the several parts of the supplicatory declamation.* London.

ANON. 1604. *Relacion de la Jornada del E. Condestable de Castilla a las pazes entre Espana e Inglaterra que concluyeron y se juraron en Londres, por el mes de Agosto anno MDCIIII* (Antwerp).

ANON. 1604. *Relacion de la Buelta del E. Condestable de Castilla de las Pazes entre Espana e Inglaterra y concordia de las placartes entre Espana y Francia* (Milan).

ANON. 1605. *The Royal Entertainement of the Right Honorable, the Earle of Nottingham, sent Ambassador from his Maiestie to the King of Spaine.* London.

ANON. 1605. *Articles of Peace, Entercourse and Commerce, concluded in the names of most high and mighty kings and Princes James, . . . and Philip the Third . . . and Albertus and Isabella Clara Eugenia . . . in a treatie at London the 18 day of August after the old stile in the yeere of our lord God 1604.* London.

COLLETON, JOHN. 1604. *A Supplication to the Kinges most Excellent Maiestie Wherein Several Reasons of State and Religion are briefly touched, not unworthie to be read and pondered by the Lords, Knights and Burgeses of the present Parliament* (London).

LECEY, JOHN. 1604. *A Petition Apologeticall Presented to the Kinges most excellent Maiesty by the Lay Catholikes of England in July last* (England).

MURIELL, CHRISTOPHER. 1603. *An Answer to the Catholiques Supplication presented unto the Kinges Majestie for a tolleration of Popish Religion in England, Wherein is contained a Confutation of their unreasonable petitions and slanderous lyes against our late Soueraigne Queene Elizabeth, whose happie and gratious gouernement the Papist in their said supplication do so peremptorilie traduce* (London).

PERSONS, ROBERT. 1602. *A Manifestation of the Great folly and bad spirit of certayne in England calling themselves secular priests* (Antwerp).

—— 1593. *Newes from Spaine and Holland: conteyning an information of Inglish affayres in Spayne with a conference therupon in Amsterdame of Holland* (Antwerp).

POWELL, GABRIEL. 1603. *The Catholikes Supplication unto the Kinges majestie for the tolleration of Catholike Religion in England* (London)

—— 1604. *A Consideration of the Papists Reasons of State and Religion for toleration of Poperie in England, intimated in their Supplication unto the Kings majestie and the States of the present Parliament* (Oxford).

SUTCLIFFE, MATTHEW. 1606. *The Petition Apologeticall of Lay Papists calling themselves the lay Catholikes of England* (London).

TRESWELL, ROBERT. 1605. *A relation of such things observed to happen in the Journey of the right Honourable Charles, Earle of Nottingham, L. High Admiral of England, His Highnesse Ambassadour to the king of Spaine* (London).

PRINTED COLLECTIONS

ANON. 1803–. *The Journals of the House of Commons* (17 v., London).

ALBA, DUQUE DE, et alii. 1936–. *Documentos Inéditos para la historia de Espana* (11 v.).

ALBERTI, L. DE, AND A. B. CHAPMAN. 1912. *English Merchants and the Spanish Inquisition in the Canaries, 1586–1594,* Royal Historical Society, 3rd ser. **23**.

BIRCH, T. 1749. *An Historical View of the Negotiations between the Courts of England, France and Brussels 1592 to 1617* (London).

BRUCE, J. 1861. *Correspondence of King James VI of Scotland and with Sir Robert Cecil and others in England* (Camden Society) **78**.

BROWN, H. F. 1898–1905. *Calendar of State Papers and manuscripts relating to English Affairs existing in the Archives . . . of Venice . . .* **9**, (1592–1603); **10**, (1603–1607); **11**, 1607–1610); **12**, (1610–1613). London.

DASENT, J. R., AND J. V. LYLE. 1890–. *Acts of the Privy Council, 1542–1628* (43 v.).

GREEN, MRS. EVERETT. 1857–. *Calendar of State Papers, Domestic . . . Elizabeth and James I . . .* **6** (1601–1603); **8** (1603–1610); **11** (1623–1625); **12** (addenda 1580–1625) (London).

HISTORICAL MANUSCRIPTS COMMISSION. 1895–. *Salisbury MSS at Hatfield House* (19 v.).

HOUSSAIE, AMELOT DE LA. 1732. *Lettres du Cardinal d'Ossat* (5 v., Amsterdam).

HUME, M. A. S. 1896–1899. *Calendar of Letters and Papers relating to English Affairs preserved principally in the Archives of Simancas* **3** (1580–1586); **4** (1587–1603) (London).

KERVYN DE LETTENHOVE, J. M. 1882–1900. *Relations Politiques des Pays Bas et de l'Angleterre* (11 v., Brussels).

LONCHAY, H., J. CUVELIER, and L. LEFEVRE. 1923–1930. *Correspondance de la Cour d'Espagne sur les affaires des Pays Bas XVII . . .*

RYMER, T., R. SANDERSON, and G. HOLMES. 1727–1729. *Foedera, Conventiones, Litterae et ciuscumque generis acta publica inter reges Angliae et alios quovis imperatores, reges, pontifices, principes, vel communitates* (17 v., London).

(Sadler Papers) SCOTT, W., ed. 1809. *State Papers and Letters of Sir Ralph Sadler* (2 v., Edinburgh).

(Sidney Papers) COLLINS, A., ed. 1746. *Letters and memorials of State . . . transcribed from the originals at Penshurst Place . . . and His Majesty's Office of Papers and Records* (2 v., London).

STEELE, ROBERT, ed. 1914. *Tudor and Stuart Proclamations 1485–1714* (2 v., Oxford).

WINWOOD, RALPH. 1725. *Memorials of Affairs of State in the reigns of Queen Elizabeth and King James* (3 v., London).

PERIODICALS, TRANSACTIONS AND SECONDARY WORKS

ALLISON, A. F., and D. M. ROGERS. 1956. "A Catalogue of Catholic Books in English Printed Abroad or Secretly in England, 1558–1640," *Biographical Studies* **3**: pp. 1–187.

DIETZ, F. C. 1923. "The Exchequer in Elizabeth's Reign," *Smith College Studies in History* **8**.

—— 1928. "The Receipts and Issue of the Exchequer during the Reigns of James I and Charles I." *Ibid.* **13**.

—— 1932. *English Public Finance, 1558–1641.* New York.

GARDINER, S. R. 1884–1886. *History of England, 1603–1642* (10 v., London).

HICKS, L. 1957. "Father Robert Persons and the *Book* of Succession," *Recusant History* **4**: pp. 104–137.

—— 1959–1960, 1962. "The Embassy of Sir Anthony Standen in 1603." *Ibid.* **5**: pp. 91–127, 184–222, **6**: pp. 163–194.

HINOJOSA, R. D. DE. 1896. *Los Despachos de la Diplomacia Pontificia en España.* (Madrid).

KERR, S. P. 1957. "The Constable Kept an Account." *Notes and Queries* **212**: 167–170.

LECLER, J. 1955. *Histoire de la Tolérance au siècle de la Réforme* (2 v., Paris; English translation, 1960).

LOOMIE, A. J. 1963. *The Spanish Elizabethans: Studies in the English Exiles at the Court of Philip II* (New York).

MEYER, A. O. 1904. "Clemens VIII and Jacob I von England," *Quellen und Forschungen aus Italienischen Archiven und Bibliotheken* **7**: 286–306.

SALYER, J. C. 1950. "Algunos Aspectos del Tratado de paz entre Inglaterra y España del Año 1604," *Simancas* **1**: 371–382.